ANTONY CLEOPATRA

WILLIAM SHAKESPEARE

Published by True Sign Publishing House
Address: SY. No. 21/2 & 21/3, Sonnenahalli,
Krishnarajapura, Bengaluru,
Karnataka - 560049 India
E-mail: truesignbooks@gmail.com
Website: www.truesign.in

Antony Cleopatra
Author: William Shakespeare

ISBN: 978-93-5462-719-4

First Edition: 2022

Contents

Dramatis Personæ

MARK ANTONY	Triumvir
OCTAVIUS CAESAR	Triumvir
LEPIDUS	Triumvir
SEXTUS POMPEIUS,	
DOMITIUS ENOBARBUS	friend to Antony
VENTIDIUS	friend to Antony
EROS	friend to Antony
SCARUS	friend to Antony
DERCETUS	friend to Antony
DEMETRIUS	friend to Antony
PHILO	friend to Antony
MAECENAS	friend to Caesar
AGRIPPA	friend to Caesar
DOLABELLA	friend to Caesar
PROCULEIUS	friend to Caesar
THIDIAS	friend to Caesar
GALLUS	friend to Caesar
MENAS	friend to Pompey
MENECRATES	friend to Pompey
VARRIUS	friend to Pompey
TAURUS	Lieutenant-General to Caesar
CANIDIUS	Lieutenant-General to Antony
SILIUS	an Officer in Ventidius's army
EUPHRONIUS	an Ambassador from Antony to Caesar
ALEXAS	attendant on Cleopatra
MARDIAN	attendant on Cleopatra
SELEUCUS	attendant on Cleopatra

DIOMEDES	attendant on Cleopatra
A SOOTHSAYER A CLOWN	
CLEOPATRA	Queen of Egypt
OCTAVIA	sister to Caesar and wife to Antony
CHARMIAN	Attendant on Cleopatra
IRAS	Attendant on Cleopatra
Officers,	
Soldiers,	
Messengers, and	
other Attendants	

SCENE: Dispersed, in several parts of the Roman Empire.

ACT-I

SCENE-I — Alexandria. A Room in Cleopatra's palace

Enter DEMETRIUS *and* PHILO.

PHILO

Nay, but this dotage of our general's
O'erflows the measure. Those his goodly eyes,
That o'er the files and musters of the war
Have glowed like plated Mars, now bend, now turn
The office and devotion of their view
Upon a tawny front. His captain's heart,
Which in the scuffles of great fights hath burst
The buckles on his breast, reneges all temper
And is become the bellows and the fan
To cool a gipsy's lust.

Flourish. Enter ANTONY *and* CLEOPATRA, *her Ladies, the Train, with Eunuchs fanning her.*

Look where they come:
Take but good note, and you shall see in him
The triple pillar of the world transform'd
Into a strumpet's fool. Behold and see.

CLEOPATRA

If it be love indeed, tell me how much.

ANTONY

There's beggary in the love that can be reckoned.

CLEOPATRA

I'll set a bourn how far to be beloved.

ANTONY

Then must thou needs find out new heaven, new earth.

Enter a MESSENGER.

MESSENGER News, my good lord, from Rome.

ANTONY Grates me, the sum.

CLEOPATRA Nay, hear them, Antony.
Fulvia perchance is angry; or who knows
If the scarce-bearded Caesar have not sent
His powerful mandate to you: "Do this or this;
Take in that kingdom and enfranchise that.
Perform't, or else we damn thee."

ANTONY How, my love?

CLEOPATRA Perchance! Nay, and most like.
You must not stay here longer; your dismission
Is come from Caesar; therefore hear it, Antony.
Where's Fulvia's process?—Caesar's I would say? Both?
Call in the messengers. As I am Egypt's queen,
Thou blushest, Antony, and that blood of thine
Is Caesar's homager; else so thy cheek pays shame
When shrill-tongued Fulvia scolds. The messengers!

ANTONY Let Rome in Tiber melt, and the wide arch
Of the ranged empire fall! Here is my space.
Kingdoms are clay. Our dungy earth alike
Feeds beast as man. The nobleness of life
Is to do thus [*Embracing*]; when such a mutual pair
And such a twain can do't, in which I bind,
On pain of punishment, the world to weet
We stand up peerless.

CLEOPATRA Excellent falsehood!
Why did he marry Fulvia, and not love her?
I'll seem the fool I am not. Antony
Will be himself.

ANTONY But stirred by Cleopatra.
Now, for the love of Love and her soft hours,
Let's not confound the time with conference harsh.

There's not a minute of our lives should stretch
Without some pleasure now. What sport tonight?

CLEOPATRA Hear the ambassadors.

ANTONY Fie, wrangling queen!
Whom everything becomes—to chide, to laugh,
To weep; whose every passion fully strives
To make itself, in thee fair and admired!
No messenger but thine, and all alone
Tonight we'll wander through the streets and note
The qualities of people. Come, my queen,
Last night you did desire it. Speak not to us.

[*Exeunt* ANTONY *and* CLEOPATRA *with the Train.*]

DEMETRIUS Is Caesar with Antonius prized so slight?

PHILO Sir, sometimes when he is not Antony,
He comes too short of that great property
Which still should go with Antony.

DEMETRIUS I am full sorry
That he approves the common liar who
Thus speaks of him at Rome, but I will hope
Of better deeds tomorrow. Rest you happy!

[*Exeunt.*]

SCENE-II — Alexandria. Another Room in Cleopatra's palace

Enter ENOBARBUS, *a* SOOTHSAYER, CHARMIAN, IRAS, MARDIAN *and* ALEXAS.

CHARMIAN: Lord Alexas, sweet Alexas, most anything Alexas, almost most absolute Alexas, where's the soothsayer that you praised so to th' queen? O, that I knew this husband which you say must charge his horns with garlands!

ALEXAS: Soothsayer!

SOOTHSAYER: Your will?

CHARMIAN: Is this the man? Is't you, sir, that know things?

SOOTHSAYER: In nature's infinite book of secrecy
A little I can read.

ALEXAS: Show him your hand.

ENOBARBUS: Bring in the banquet quickly; wine enough
Cleopatra's health to drink.

CHARMIAN: Good, sir, give me good fortune.

SOOTHSAYER: I make not, but foresee.

CHARMIAN: Pray, then, foresee me one.

SOOTHSAYER: You shall be yet far fairer than you are.

CHARMIAN: He means in flesh.

IRAS: No, you shall paint when you are old.

CHARMIAN: Wrinkles forbid!

ALEXAS: Vex not his prescience. Be attentive.

CHARMIAN: Hush!

SOOTHSAYER: You shall be more beloving than beloved.

CHARMIAN: I had rather heat my liver with drinking.

ALEXAS	Nay, hear him.
CHARMIAN	Good now, some excellent fortune! Let me be married to three kings in a forenoon and widow them all. Let me have a child at fifty, to whom Herod of Jewry may do homage. Find me to marry me with Octavius Caesar, and companion me with my mistress.
SOOTHSAYER	You shall outlive the lady whom you serve.
CHARMIAN	O, excellent! I love long life better than figs.
SOOTHSAYER	You have seen and proved a fairer former fortune Than that which is to approach.
CHARMIAN	Then belike my children shall have no names. Prithee, how many boys and wenches must I have?
SOOTHSAYER	If every of your wishes had a womb, And fertile every wish, a million.
CHARMIAN	Out, fool! I forgive thee for a witch.
ALEXAS	You think none but your sheets are privy to your wishes.
CHARMIAN	Nay, come, tell Iras hers.
ALEXAS	We'll know all our fortunes.
ENOBARBUS	Mine, and most of our fortunes tonight, shall be drunk to bed.
IRAS	There's a palm presages chastity, if nothing else.
CHARMIAN	E'en as the o'erflowing Nilus presageth famine.
IRAS	Go, you wild bedfellow, you cannot soothsay.
CHARMIAN	Nay, if an oily palm be not a fruitful prognostication, I cannot scratch mine ear. Prithee, tell her but workaday fortune.
SOOTHSAYER	Your fortunes are alike.
IRAS	But how, but how? give me particulars.
SOOTHSAYER	I have said.
IRAS	Am I not an inch of fortune better than she?
CHARMIAN	Well, if you were but an inch of fortune better than I, where would you choose it?

IRAS — Not in my husband's nose.

CHARMIAN — Our worser thoughts heavens mend! Alexas—come, his fortune! his fortune! O, let him marry a woman that cannot go, sweet Isis, I beseech thee, and let her die too, and give him a worse, and let worse follow worse, till the worst of all follow him laughing to his grave, fiftyfold a cuckold! Good Isis, hear me this prayer, though thou deny me a matter of more weight; good Isis, I beseech thee!

IRAS — Amen. Dear goddess, hear that prayer of the people! For, as it is a heartbreaking to see a handsome man loose-wived, so it is a deadly sorrow to behold a foul knave uncuckolded. Therefore, dear Isis, keep decorum and fortune him accordingly!

CHARMIAN — Amen.

ALEXAS — Lo now, if it lay in their hands to make me a cuckold, they would make themselves whores but they'd do't!

Enter CLEOPATRA.

ENOBARBUS — Hush, Here comes Antony.

CHARMIAN — Not he, the queen.

CLEOPATRA — Saw you my lord?

ENOBARBUS — No, lady.

CLEOPATRA — Was he not here?

CHARMIAN — No, madam.

CLEOPATRA — He was disposed to mirth; but on the sudden
A Roman thought hath struck him. Enobarbus!

ENOBARBUS — Madam?

CLEOPATRA — Seek him and bring him hither. Where's Alexas?

ALEXAS — Here, at your service. My lord approaches.

Enter ANTONY *with a* MESSENGER.

CLEOPATRA — We will not look upon him. Go with us.

[*Exeunt* CLEOPATRA, ENOBARBUS, CHARMIAN, IRAS, ALEXAS *and* SOOTHSAYER.]

MESSENGER Fulvia thy wife first came into the field.

ANTONY Against my brother Lucius.

MESSENGER Ay.
But soon that war had end, and the time's state
Made friends of them, jointing their force
'gainst Caesar,
Whose better issue in the war from Italy
Upon the first encounter drave them.

ANTONY Well, what worst?

MESSENGER The nature of bad news infects the teller.

ANTONY When it concerns the fool or coward. On.
Things that are past are done with me. 'Tis thus:
Who tells me true, though in his tale lie death,
I hear him as he flattered.

MESSENGER Labienus—
This is stiff news—hath with his Parthian force
Extended Asia from Euphrates
His conquering banner shook from Syria
To Lydia and to Ionia,
Whilst—

ANTONY "Antony", thou wouldst say—

MESSENGER O, my lord!

ANTONY Speak to me home; mince not the general
tongue.
Name Cleopatra as she is called in Rome;
Rail thou in Fulvia's phrase, and taunt my faults
With such full licence as both truth and malice
Have power to utter. O, then we bring forth
weeds
When our quick minds lie still, and our ills told
us
Is as our earing. Fare thee well awhile.

MESSENGER At your noble pleasure.

[*Exit* MESSENGER.]

Enter another MESSENGER.

ANTONY From Sicyon, ho, the news? Speak there!

SECOND MESSENGER The man from Sicyon—

ANTONY Is there such a one?

SECOND MESSENGER He stays upon your will.

ANTONY Let him appear.

[*Exit second* MESSENGER.]

These strong Egyptian fetters I must break,
Or lose myself in dotage.

Enter another MESSENGER *with a letter.*

What are you?

THIRD MESSENGER Fulvia thy wife is dead.

ANTONY Where died she?

THIRD MESSENGER In Sicyon:
Her length of sickness, with what else more serious
Importeth thee to know, this bears.

[*Gives a letter.*]

ANTONY Forbear me.

[*Exit third* MESSENGER.]

There's a great spirit gone! Thus did I desire it.
What our contempts doth often hurl from us,
We wish it ours again. The present pleasure,
By revolution lowering, does become
The opposite of itself. She's good, being gone.
The hand could pluck her back that shoved her on.
I must from this enchanting queen break off.
Ten thousand harms, more than the ills I know,
My idleness doth hatch. How now, Enobarbus!

Enter ENOBARBUS.

ENOBARBUS What's your pleasure, sir?

ANTONY I must with haste from hence.

ENOBARBUS Why then we kill all our women. We see how mortal an unkindness is to them. If they suffer our departure, death's the word.

ANTONY I must be gone.

ENOBARBUS Under a compelling occasion, let women die. It were pity to cast them away for nothing, though, between them and a great cause they should be esteemed nothing. Cleopatra, catching but the least noise of this, dies instantly. I have seen her die twenty times upon far poorer moment. I do think there is mettle in death which commits some loving act upon her, she hath such a celerity in dying.

ANTONY She is cunning past man's thought.

ENOBARBUS Alack, sir, no; her passions are made of nothing but the finest part of pure love. We cannot call her winds and waters sighs and tears; they are greater storms and tempests than almanacs can report. This cannot be cunning in her; if it be, she makes a shower of rain as well as Jove.

ANTONY Would I had never seen her!

ENOBARBUS O, sir, you had then left unseen a wonderful piece of work, which not to have been blest withal would have discredited your travel.

ANTONY Fulvia is dead.

ENOBARBUS Sir?

ANTONY Fulvia is dead.

ENOBARBUS Fulvia?

ANTONY Dead.

ENOBARBUS Why, sir, give the gods a thankful sacrifice. When it pleaseth their deities to take the wife of a man from him, it shows to man the tailors of the earth; comforting therein that when old robes are worn out, there are members to make new. If there were no more women but Fulvia, then had you indeed a cut, and the case to be lamented. This grief is crowned with consolation; your old smock brings forth a new petticoat: and indeed the tears live in an onion that should water this sorrow.

ANTONY

The business she hath broached in the state
Cannot endure my absence.

ENOBARBUS

And the business you have broached here cannot be without you, especially that of Cleopatra's, which wholly depends on your abode.

ANTONY

No more light answers. Let our officers
Have notice what we purpose. I shall break
The cause of our expedience to the Queen,
And get her leave to part. For not alone
The death of Fulvia, with more urgent touches,
Do strongly speak to us, but the letters too
Of many our contriving friends in Rome
Petition us at home. Sextus Pompeius
Hath given the dare to Caesar, and commands
The empire of the sea. Our slippery people,
Whose love is never linked to the deserver
Till his deserts are past, begin to throw
Pompey the Great and all his dignities
Upon his son, who, high in name and power,
Higher than both in blood and life, stands up
For the main soldier; whose quality, going on,
The sides o' th' world may danger. Much is breeding
Which, like the courser's hair, hath yet but life
And not a serpent's poison. Say our pleasure
To such whose place is under us, requires
Our quick remove from hence.

ENOBARBUS

I shall do't.

[*Exeunt.*]

SCENE-III — Alexandria. A Room in Cleopatra's palace

Enter CLEOPATRA, CHARMIAN, ALEXAS *and* IRAS.

CLEOPATRA — Where is he?

CHARMIAN — I did not see him since.

CLEOPATRA — See where he is, who's with him, what he does.
I did not send you. If you find him sad,
Say I am dancing; if in mirth, report
That I am sudden sick. Quick, and return.

[*Exit* ALEXAS.]

CHARMIAN — Madam, methinks, if you did love him dearly,
You do not hold the method to enforce
The like from him.

CLEOPATRA — What should I do I do not?

CHARMIAN — In each thing give him way; cross him in nothing.

CLEOPATRA — Thou teachest like a fool: the way to lose him.

CHARMIAN — Tempt him not so too far; I wish, forbear.
In time we hate that which we often fear.
But here comes Antony.

Enter ANTONY.

CLEOPATRA — I am sick and sullen.

ANTONY — I am sorry to give breathing to my purpose—

CLEOPATRA — Help me away, dear Charmian! I shall fall.
It cannot be thus long; the sides of nature
Will not sustain it.

ANTONY — Now, my dearest queen—

CLEOPATRA — Pray you, stand farther from me.

ANTONY What's the matter?

CLEOPATRA I know by that same eye there's some good news.
What, says the married woman you may go?
Would she had never given you leave to come!
Let her not say 'tis I that keep you here.
I have no power upon you; hers you are.

ANTONY The gods best know—

CLEOPATRA O, never was there queen
So mightily betrayed! Yet at the first
I saw the treasons planted.

ANTONY Cleopatra—

CLEOPATRA Why should I think you can be mine and true,
Though you in swearing shake the throned gods,
Who have been false to Fulvia? Riotous madness,
To be entangled with those mouth-made vows
Which break themselves in swearing!

ANTONY Most sweet queen—

CLEOPATRA Nay, pray you seek no colour for your going,
But bid farewell and go. When you sued staying,
Then was the time for words. No going then,
Eternity was in our lips and eyes,
Bliss in our brows' bent; none our parts so poor
But was a race of heaven. They are so still,
Or thou, the greatest soldier of the world,
Art turned the greatest liar.

ANTONY How now, lady!

CLEOPATRA I would I had thy inches, thou shouldst know
There were a heart in Egypt.

ANTONY Hear me, queen:
The strong necessity of time commands
Our services awhile, but my full heart
Remains in use with you. Our Italy
Shines o'er with civil swords; Sextus Pompeius
Makes his approaches to the port of Rome;
Equality of two domestic powers

Breed scrupulous faction; the hated, grown to strength,
Are newly grown to love; the condemned Pompey,
Rich in his father's honour, creeps apace
Into the hearts of such as have not thrived
Upon the present state, whose numbers threaten;
And quietness, grown sick of rest, would purge
By any desperate change. My more particular,
And that which most with you should safe my going,
Is Fulvia's death.

CLEOPATRA Though age from folly could not give me freedom,
It does from childishness. Can Fulvia die?

ANTONY She's dead, my queen.
Look here, and at thy sovereign leisure read
The garboils she awaked; at the last, best,
See when and where she died.

CLEOPATRA O most false love!
Where be the sacred vials thou shouldst fill
With sorrowful water? Now I see, I see,
In Fulvia's death how mine received shall be.

ANTONY Quarrel no more, but be prepared to know
The purposes I bear; which are, or cease,
As you shall give th' advice. By the fire
That quickens Nilus' slime, I go from hence
Thy soldier, servant, making peace or war
As thou affects.

CLEOPATRA Cut my lace, Charmian, come!
But let it be; I am quickly ill and well,
So Antony loves.

ANTONY My precious queen, forbear,
And give true evidence to his love, which stands
An honourable trial.

CLEOPATRA So Fulvia told me.
I prithee, turn aside and weep for her,
Then bid adieu to me, and say the tears

Belong to Egypt. Good now, play one scene
Of excellent dissembling, and let it look
Like perfect honour.

ANTONY You'll heat my blood. No more.

CLEOPATRA You can do better yet, but this is meetly.

ANTONY Now, by my sword—

CLEOPATRA And target. Still he mends.
But this is not the best. Look, prithee, Charmian,
How this Herculean Roman does become
The carriage of his chafe.

ANTONY I'll leave you, lady.

CLEOPATRA Courteous lord, one word.
Sir, you and I must part, but that's not it;
Sir, you and I have loved, but there's not it;
That you know well. Something it is I would—
O, my oblivion is a very Antony,
And I am all forgotten.

ANTONY But that your royalty
Holds idleness your subject, I should take you
For idleness itself.

CLEOPATRA 'Tis sweating labour
To bear such idleness so near the heart
As Cleopatra this. But, sir, forgive me,
Since my becomings kill me when they do not
Eye well to you. Your honour calls you hence;
Therefore be deaf to my unpitied folly,
And all the gods go with you! Upon your sword
Sit laurel victory, and smooth success
Be strewed before your feet!

ANTONY Let us go. Come.
Our separation so abides and flies
That thou, residing here, goes yet with me,
And I, hence fleeting, here remain with thee.
Away!

[*Exeunt.*]

SCENE-IV — Rome. An Apartment in Caesar's House

Enter Octavius [Caesar], Lepidus *and their train.*

CAESAR
You may see, Lepidus, and henceforth know,
It is not Caesar's natural vice to hate
Our great competitor. From Alexandria
This is the news: he fishes, drinks, and wastes
The lamps of night in revel: is not more manlike
Than Cleopatra, nor the queen of Ptolemy
More womanly than he; hardly gave audience, or
Vouchsafed to think he had partners. You shall find there
A man who is the abstract of all faults
That all men follow.

LEPIDUS
I must not think there are
Evils enough to darken all his goodness.
His faults in him seem as the spots of heaven,
More fiery by night's blackness; hereditary
Rather than purchased; what he cannot change
Than what he chooses.

CAESAR
You are too indulgent. Let's grant it is not
Amiss to tumble on the bed of Ptolemy,
To give a kingdom for a mirth, to sit
And keep the turn of tippling with a slave,

To reel the streets at noon, and stand the buffet
With knaves that smell of sweat. Say this becomes him—
As his composure must be rare indeed
Whom these things cannot blemish—yet must Antony
No way excuse his foils when we do bear
So great weight in his lightness. If he filled
His vacancy with his voluptuousness,
Full surfeits and the dryness of his bones
Call on him for't. But to confound such time
That drums him from his sport, and speaks as loud
As his own state and ours, 'tis to be chid
As we rate boys who, being mature in knowledge,
Pawn their experience to their present pleasure
And so rebel to judgment.

Enter a MESSENGER.

LEPIDUS	Here's more news.
MESSENGER	Thy biddings have been done, and every hour, Most noble Caesar, shalt thou have report How 'tis abroad. Pompey is strong at sea, And it appears he is beloved of those That only have feared Caesar. To the ports The discontents repair, and men's reports Give him much wronged.
CAESAR	I should have known no less. It hath been taught us from the primal state That he which is was wished until he were, And the ebbed man, ne'er loved till ne'er worth love, Comes deared by being lacked. This common body, Like to a vagabond flag upon the stream, Goes to and back, lackeying the varying

tide,
To rot itself with motion.

Enter a second MESSENGER.

SECOND MESSENGER Caesar, I bring thee word
Menecrates and Menas, famous pirates,
Make the sea serve them, which they ear and wound
With keels of every kind. Many hot inroads
They make in Italy—the borders maritime
Lack blood to think on't—and flush youth revolt.
No vessel can peep forth but 'tis as soon
Taken as seen; for Pompey's name strikes more
Than could his war resisted.

CAESAR Antony,
Leave thy lascivious wassails. When thou once
Was beaten from Modena, where thou slew'st
Hirtius and Pansa, consuls, at thy heel
Did famine follow, whom thou fought'st against,
Though daintily brought up, with patience more
Than savages could suffer. Thou didst drink
The stale of horses and the gilded puddle
Which beasts would cough at. Thy palate then did deign
The roughest berry on the rudest hedge.
Yea, like the stag when snow the pasture sheets,
The barks of trees thou browsed. On the Alps
It is reported thou didst eat strange flesh
Which some did die to look on. And all this—
It wounds thine honour that I speak it now—

Was borne so like a soldier that thy cheek
So much as lanked not.

LEPIDUS 'Tis pity of him.

CAESAR Let his shames quickly
Drive him to Rome. 'Tis time we twain
Did show ourselves i' th' field, and to that end
Assemble we immediate council. Pompey
Thrives in our idleness.

LEPIDUS Tomorrow, Caesar,
I shall be furnished to inform you rightly
Both what by sea and land I can be able
To front this present time.

CAESAR Till which encounter
It is my business too. Farewell.

LEPIDUS Farewell, my lord. What you shall know meantime
Of stirs abroad, I shall beseech you, sir,
To let me be partaker.

CAESAR Doubt not, sir.
I knew it for my bond.

[*Exeunt.*]

SCENE-V — Alexandria. A Room in the Palace

Enter CLEOPATRA, CHARMIAN, IRAS *and* MARDIAN.

CLEOPATRA Charmian!

CHARMIAN Madam?

CLEOPATRA Ha, ha!
Give me to drink mandragora.

CHARMIAN Why, madam?

CLEOPATRA That I might sleep out this great gap of time
My Antony is away.

CHARMIAN You think of him too much.

CLEOPATRA O, 'tis treason!

CHARMIAN Madam, I trust not so.

CLEOPATRA Thou, eunuch Mardian!

MARDIAN What's your highness' pleasure?

CLEOPATRA Not now to hear thee sing. I take no pleasure
In aught an eunuch has. 'Tis well for thee
That, being unseminared, thy freer thoughts
May not fly forth of Egypt. Hast thou
affections?

MARDIAN Yes, gracious madam.

CLEOPATRA Indeed?

MARDIAN Not in deed, madam, for I can do nothing
But what indeed is honest to be done.
Yet have I fierce affections, and think
What Venus did with Mars.

CLEOPATRA O, Charmian,
Where think'st thou he is now? Stands he, or
sits he?

Or does he walk? Or is he on his horse?
O happy horse, to bear the weight of Antony!
Do bravely, horse, for wot'st thou whom thou mov'st?
The demi-Atlas of this earth, the arm
And burgonet of men. He's speaking now,
Or murmuring "Where's my serpent of old Nile?"
For so he calls me. Now I feed myself
With most delicious poison. Think on me
That am with Phœbus' amorous pinches black,
And wrinkled deep in time? Broad-fronted Caesar,
When thou wast here above the ground, I was
A morsel for a monarch. And great Pompey
Would stand and make his eyes grow in my brow;
There would he anchor his aspect, and die
With looking on his life.

Enter ALEXAS.

ALEXAS
Sovereign of Egypt, hail!

CLEOPATRA
How much unlike art thou Mark Antony!
Yet, coming from him, that great medicine hath
With his tinct gilded thee.
How goes it with my brave Mark Antony?

ALEXAS
Last thing he did, dear queen,
He kissed—the last of many doubled kisses—
This orient pearl. His speech sticks in my heart.

CLEOPATRA
Mine ear must pluck it thence.

ALEXAS
"Good friend," quoth he,
"Say, the firm Roman to great Egypt sends
This treasure of an oyster; at whose foot,
To mend the petty present, I will piece
Her opulent throne with kingdoms. All the east,
Say thou, shall call her mistress." So he nodded
And soberly did mount an arm-gaunt steed,
Who neighed so high that what I would have spoke
Was beastly dumbed by him.

CLEOPATRA What, was he sad or merry?

ALEXAS Like to the time o' th' year between the extremes
Of hot and cold, he was nor sad nor merry.

CLEOPATRA O well-divided disposition!—Note him,
Note him, good Charmian, 'tis the man; but note him:
He was not sad, for he would shine on those
That make their looks by his; he was not merry,
Which seemed to tell them his remembrance lay
In Egypt with his joy; but between both.
O heavenly mingle!—Be'st thou sad or merry,
The violence of either thee becomes,
So does it no man else.—Met'st thou my posts?

ALEXAS Ay, madam, twenty several messengers.
Why do you send so thick?

CLEOPATRA Who's born that day
When I forget to send to Antony
Shall die a beggar.—Ink and paper, Charmian.—
Welcome, my good Alexas.—Did I, Charmian,
Ever love Caesar so?

CHARMIAN O that brave Caesar!

CLEOPATRA Be choked with such another emphasis!
Say "the brave Antony."

CHARMIAN The valiant Caesar!

CLEOPATRA By Isis, I will give thee bloody teeth
If thou with Caesar paragon again
My man of men.

CHARMIAN By your most gracious pardon,
I sing but after you.

CLEOPATRA My salad days,
When I was green in judgment, cold in blood,
To say as I said then. But come, away,
Get me ink and paper.
He shall have every day a several greeting,
Or I'll unpeople Egypt.

[*Exeunt.*]

ACT-II

SCENE-I — Messina. A Room in Pompey's house

Enter POMPEY, MENECRATES *and* MENAS *in warlike manner.*

POMPEY
If the great gods be just, they shall assist
The deeds of justest men.

MENECRATES
Know, worthy Pompey,
That what they do delay they not deny.

POMPEY
Whiles we are suitors to their throne, decays
The thing we sue for.

MENECRATES
We, ignorant of ourselves,
Beg often our own harms, which the wise powers
Deny us for our good; so find we profit
By losing of our prayers.

POMPEY
I shall do well.
The people love me, and the sea is mine;
My powers are crescent, and my auguring hope
Says it will come to th' full. Mark Antony
In Egypt sits at dinner, and will make
No wars without doors. Caesar gets money where
He loses hearts. Lepidus flatters both,
Of both is flattered; but he neither loves
Nor either cares for him.

MENAS
Caesar and Lepidus
Are in the field. A mighty strength they carry.

POMPEY
Where have you this? 'Tis false.

MENAS
From Silvius, sir.

POMPEY He dreams. I know they are in Rome together,
Looking for Antony. But all the charms of love,
Salt Cleopatra, soften thy waned lip!
Let witchcraft join with beauty, lust with both;
Tie up the libertine in a field of feasts;
Keep his brain fuming. Epicurean cooks
Sharpen with cloyless sauce his appetite,
That sleep and feeding may prorogue his honour
Even till a Lethe'd dullness—

Enter VARRIUS.

How now, Varrius!

VARRIUS This is most certain that I shall deliver:
Mark Antony is every hour in Rome
Expected. Since he went from Egypt 'tis
A space for farther travel.

POMPEY I could have given less matter
A better ear.—Menas, I did not think
This amorous surfeiter would have donned his helm
For such a petty war. His soldiership
Is twice the other twain. But let us rear
The higher our opinion, that our stirring
Can from the lap of Egypt's widow pluck
The ne'er lust-wearied Antony.

MENAS I cannot hope
Caesar and Antony shall well greet together.
His wife that's dead did trespasses to Caesar;
His brother warred upon him, although I think,
Not moved by Antony.

POMPEY I know not, Menas,
How lesser enmities may give way to greater.
Were't not that we stand up against them all,
'Twere pregnant they should square between themselves,
For they have entertained cause enough
To draw their swords. But how the fear of us
May cement their divisions, and bind up
The petty difference, we yet not know.

Be't as our gods will have't! It only stands
Our lives upon to use our strongest hands.
Come, Menas.

[*Exeunt.*]

SCENE-II — Rome. A Room in the House of Lepidus

Enter ENOBARBUS *and* LEPIDUS.

LEPIDUS
Good Enobarbus, 'tis a worthy deed,
And shall become you well, to entreat your captain
To soft and gentle speech.

ENOBARBUS
I shall entreat him
To answer like himself. If Caesar move him,
Let Antony look over Caesar's head
And speak as loud as Mars. By Jupiter,
Were I the wearer of Antonius' beard,
I would not shave't today.

LEPIDUS
'Tis not a time
For private stomaching.

ENOBARBUS
Every time
Serves for the matter that is then born in't.

LEPIDUS
But small to greater matters must give way.

ENOBARBUS
Not if the small come first.

LEPIDUS
Your speech is passion;
But pray you stir no embers up. Here comes
The noble Antony.

Enter ANTONY *and* VENTIDIUS.

ENOBARBUS
And yonder Caesar.

Enter CAESAR, MAECENAS *and* AGRIPPA.

ANTONY
If we compose well here, to Parthia.
Hark, Ventidius.

CAESAR
I do not know, Maecenas. Ask Agrippa.

LEPIDUS — Noble friends,
That which combined us was most great, and let not
A leaner action rend us. What's amiss,
May it be gently heard. When we debate
Our trivial difference loud, we do commit
Murder in healing wounds. Then, noble partners,
The rather for I earnestly beseech,
Touch you the sourest points with sweetest terms,
Nor curstness grow to th' matter.

ANTONY — 'Tis spoken well.
Were we before our armies, and to fight,
I should do thus.

CAESAR — Welcome to Rome.

ANTONY — Thank you.

CAESAR — Sit.

ANTONY — Sit, sir.

CAESAR — Nay, then.

ANTONY — I learn you take things ill which are not so,
Or being, concern you not.

CAESAR — I must be laughed at
If, or for nothing or a little, I
Should say myself offended, and with you
Chiefly i' th' world; more laughed at that I should
Once name you derogately when to sound your name
It not concerned me.

ANTONY — My being in Egypt, Caesar,
What was't to you?

CAESAR — No more than my residing here at Rome
Might be to you in Egypt. Yet if you there
Did practise on my state, your being in Egypt
Might be my question.

ANTONY — How intend you, practised?

CAESAR You may be pleased to catch at mine intent
By what did here befall me. Your wife and brother
Made wars upon me, and their contestation
Was theme for you; you were the word of war.

ANTONY You do mistake your business. My brother never
Did urge me in his act. I did inquire it,
And have my learning from some true reports
That drew their swords with you. Did he not rather
Discredit my authority with yours,
And make the wars alike against my stomach,
Having alike your cause? Of this my letters
Before did satisfy you. If you'll patch a quarrel,
As matter whole you have not to make it with,
It must not be with this.

CAESAR. You praise yourself
By laying defects of judgment to me; but
You patched up your excuses.

ANTONY Not so, not so.
I know you could not lack—I am certain on't—
Very necessity of this thought, that I,
Your partner in the cause 'gainst which he fought,
Could not with graceful eyes attend those wars
Which fronted mine own peace. As for my wife,
I would you had her spirit in such another.
The third o' th' world is yours, which with a snaffle
You may pace easy, but not such a wife.

ENOBARBUS Would we had all such wives, that the men
Might go to wars with the women.

ANTONY So much uncurbable, her garboils, Caesar,
Made out of her impatience—which not wanted
Shrewdness of policy too—I grieving grant
Did you too much disquiet. For that you must
But say I could not help it.

CAESAR I wrote to you
When rioting in Alexandria; you

Did pocket up my letters, and with taunts
Did gibe my missive out of audience.

ANTONY — Sir,
He fell upon me ere admitted, then.
Three kings I had newly feasted, and did want
Of what I was i' th' morning. But next day
I told him of myself, which was as much
As to have asked him pardon. Let this fellow
Be nothing of our strife; if we contend,
Out of our question wipe him.

CAESAR — You have broken
The article of your oath, which you shall never
Have tongue to charge me with.

LEPIDUS — Soft, Caesar!

ANTONY — No, Lepidus, let him speak.
The honour is sacred which he talks on now,
Supposing that I lacked it. But on, Caesar:
The article of my oath?

CAESAR — To lend me arms and aid when I required them,
The which you both denied.

ANTONY — Neglected, rather;
And then when poisoned hours had bound me up
From mine own knowledge. As nearly as I may
I'll play the penitent to you. But mine honesty
Shall not make poor my greatness, nor my power
Work without it. Truth is that Fulvia,
To have me out of Egypt, made wars here,
For which myself, the ignorant motive, do
So far ask pardon as befits mine honour
To stoop in such a case.

LEPIDUS — 'Tis noble spoken.

MAECENAS — If it might please you to enforce no further
The griefs between ye; to forget them quite
Were to remember that the present need
Speaks to atone you.

LEPIDUS — Worthily spoken, Maecenas.

ENOBARBUS Or, if you borrow one another's love for the instant, you may, when you hear no more words of Pompey, return it again. You shall have time to wrangle in when you have nothing else to do.

ANTONY Thou art a soldier only. Speak no more.

ENOBARBUS That truth should be silent I had almost forgot.

ANTONY You wrong this presence; therefore speak no more.

ENOBARBUS Go to, then. Your considerate stone!

CAESAR I do not much dislike the matter, but
The manner of his speech; for't cannot be
We shall remain in friendship, our conditions
So differing in their acts. Yet if I knew
What hoop should hold us staunch, from edge to edge
O' th' world I would pursue it.

AGRIPPA Give me leave, Caesar.

CAESAR Speak, Agrippa.

AGRIPPA Thou hast a sister by the mother's side,
Admired Octavia. Great Mark Antony
Is now a widower.

CAESAR Say not so, Agrippa.
If Cleopatra heard you, your reproof
Were well deserved of rashness.

ANTONY I am not married, Caesar. Let me hear
Agrippa further speak.

AGRIPPA To hold you in perpetual amity,
To make you brothers, and to knit your hearts
With an unslipping knot, take Antony
Octavia to his wife; whose beauty claims
No worse a husband than the best of men;
Whose virtue and whose general graces speak
That which none else can utter. By this marriage
All little jealousies, which now seem great,
And all great fears, which now import their dangers,
Would then be nothing. Truths would be tales,
Where now half-tales be truths. Her love to

both
Would each to other, and all loves to both,
Draw after her. Pardon what I have spoke,
For 'tis a studied, not a present thought,
By duty ruminated.

ANTONY Will Caesar speak?

CAESAR Not till he hears how Antony is touched
With what is spoke already.

ANTONY What power is in Agrippa,
If I would say "Agrippa, be it so,"
To make this good?

CAESAR The power of Caesar, and
His power unto Octavia.

ANTONY May I never
To this good purpose, that so fairly shows,
Dream of impediment! Let me have thy hand.
Further this act of grace; and from this hour
The heart of brothers govern in our loves
And sway our great designs!

CAESAR There's my hand.
A sister I bequeath you, whom no brother
Did ever love so dearly. Let her live
To join our kingdoms and our hearts; and never
Fly off our loves again!

LEPIDUS Happily, amen!

ANTONY I did not think to draw my sword 'gainst
Pompey,
For he hath laid strange courtesies and great
Of late upon me. I must thank him only,
Lest my remembrance suffer ill report;
At heel of that, defy him.

LEPIDUS Time calls upon 's.
Of us must Pompey presently be sought,
Or else he seeks out us.

ANTONY Where lies he?

CAESAR About the Mount Misena.

ANTONY What is his strength by land?

CAESAR Great and increasing; but by sea
He is an absolute master.

ANTONY So is the fame.
Would we had spoke together! Haste we for it.
Yet, ere we put ourselves in arms, dispatch we
The business we have talked of.

CAESAR With most gladness,
And do invite you to my sister's view,
Whither straight I'll lead you.

ANTONY Let us, Lepidus, not lack your company.

LEPIDUS Noble Antony, not sickness should detain me.

[*Flourish. Exeunt all except* ENOBARBUS, AGRIPPA *and* MAECENAS.]

MAECENAS Welcome from Egypt, sir.

ENOBARBUS Half the heart of Caesar, worthy Maecenas! My honourable friend, Agrippa!

AGRIPPA Good Enobarbus!

MAECENAS We have cause to be glad that matters are so well digested. You stayed well by 't in Egypt.

ENOBARBUS Ay, sir, we did sleep day out of countenance and made the night light with drinking.

MAECENAS Eight wild boars roasted whole at a breakfast, and but twelve persons there. Is this true?

ENOBARBUS This was but as a fly by an eagle. We had much more monstrous matter of feast, which worthily deserved noting.

MAECENAS She's a most triumphant lady, if report be square to her.

ENOBARBUS When she first met Mark Antony, she pursed up his heart upon the river of Cydnus.

AGRIPPA There she appeared indeed, or my reporter devised well for her.

ENOBARBUS I will tell you.
The barge she sat in, like a burnished throne,
Burned on the water. The poop was beaten gold;
Purple the sails, and so perfumed that
The winds were love-sick with them; the oars

were silver,
Which to the tune of flutes kept stroke, and made
The water which they beat to follow faster,
As amorous of their strokes. For her own person,
It beggared all description: she did lie
In her pavilion, cloth-of-gold of tissue,
O'erpicturing that Venus where we see
The fancy outwork nature. On each side her
Stood pretty dimpled boys, like smiling Cupids,
With divers-coloured fans, whose wind did seem
To glow the delicate cheeks which they did cool,
And what they undid did.

AGRIPPA O, rare for Antony!

ENOBARBUS Her gentlewomen, like the Nereides,
So many mermaids, tended her i' th' eyes,
And made their bends adornings. At the helm
A seeming mermaid steers. The silken tackle
Swell with the touches of those flower-soft hands
That yarely frame the office. From the barge
A strange invisible perfume hits the sense
Of the adjacent wharfs. The city cast
Her people out upon her, and Antony,
Enthroned i' th' market-place, did sit alone,
Whistling to th' air, which, but for vacancy,
Had gone to gaze on Cleopatra too,
And made a gap in nature.

AGRIPPA Rare Egyptian!

ENOBARBUS Upon her landing, Antony sent to her,
Invited her to supper. She replied
It should be better he became her guest,
Which she entreated. Our courteous Antony,
Whom ne'er the word of "No" woman heard speak,
Being barbered ten times o'er, goes to the feast,

And, for his ordinary, pays his heart
For what his eyes eat only.

AGRIPPA
Royal wench!
She made great Caesar lay his sword to bed.
He ploughed her, and she cropped.

ENOBARBUS
I saw her once
Hop forty paces through the public street
And, having lost her breath, she spoke and panted,
That she did make defect perfection,
And, breathless, pour breath forth.

MAECENAS
Now Antony must leave her utterly.

ENOBARBUS
Never. He will not.
Age cannot wither her, nor custom stale
Her infinite variety. Other women cloy
The appetites they feed, but she makes hungry
Where most she satisfies. For vilest things
Become themselves in her, that the holy priests
Bless her when she is riggish.

MAECENAS
If beauty, wisdom, modesty can settle
The heart of Antony, Octavia is
A blessed lottery to him.

AGRIPPA
Let us go.
Good Enobarbus, make yourself my guest
Whilst you abide here.

ENOBARBUS
Humbly, sir, I thank you.

[*Exeunt.*]

SCENE-III — Rome. A Room in Caesar's House

Enter ANTONY, CAESAR, OCTAVIA *between them.*

ANTONY	The world and my great office will sometimes Divide me from your bosom.
OCTAVIA	All which time Before the gods my knee shall bow my prayers To them for you.
ANTONY	Good night, sir.—My Octavia, Read not my blemishes in the world's report. I have not kept my square, but that to come Shall all be done by th' rule. Good night, dear lady.
OCTAVIA	Good night, sir.
CAESAR	Good night.

[*Exeunt* CAESAR *and* OCTAVIA.]

Enter SOOTHSAYER.

ANTONY	Now, sirrah, you do wish yourself in Egypt?
SOOTHSAYER	Would I had never come from thence, nor you thither!
ANTONY	If you can, your reason.
SOOTHSAYER	I see it in my motion, have it not in my tongue. But yet hie you to Egypt again.
ANTONY	Say to me, Whose fortunes shall rise higher, Caesar's or mine?
SOOTHSAYER	Caesar's. Therefore, O Antony, stay not by his side.

Thy dæmon—that thy spirit which keeps thee—is
Noble, courageous, high, unmatchable,
Where Caesar's is not. But near him, thy angel
Becomes afeard, as being o'erpowered. Therefore
Make space enough between you.

ANTONY Speak this no more.

SOOTHSAYER To none but thee; no more but when to thee.
If thou dost play with him at any game,
Thou art sure to lose; and of that natural luck
He beats thee 'gainst the odds. Thy lustre thickens
When he shines by. I say again, thy spirit
Is all afraid to govern thee near him;
But, he away, 'tis noble.

ANTONY Get thee gone.
Say to Ventidius I would speak with him.

[*Exit* SOOTHSAYER.]

He shall to Parthia. Be it art or hap,
He hath spoken true. The very dice obey him,
And in our sports my better cunning faints
Under his chance. If we draw lots, he speeds;
His cocks do win the battle still of mine
When it is all to naught, and his quails ever
Beat mine, inhooped, at odds. I will to Egypt:
And though I make this marriage for my peace,
I' th' East my pleasure lies.

Enter VENTIDIUS.

O, come, Ventidius,
You must to Parthia. Your commission's ready.
Follow me and receive 't.

[*Exeunt.*]

SCENE-IV — Rome. A street

Enter LEPIDUS, MAECENAS *and* AGRIPPA.

LEPIDUS
Trouble yourselves no further. Pray you hasten
Your generals after.

AGRIPPA
Sir, Mark Antony
Will e'en but kiss Octavia, and we'll follow.

LEPIDUS
Till I shall see you in your soldier's dress,
Which will become you both, farewell.

MAECENAS
We shall,
As I conceive the journey, be at the Mount
Before you, Lepidus.

LEPIDUS
Your way is shorter;
My purposes do draw me much about.
You'll win two days upon me.

BOTH
Sir, good success!

LEPIDUS
Farewell.

[*Exeunt.*]

SCENE-V — Alexandria. A Room in the Palace

Enter CLEOPATRA, CHARMIAN, IRAS, ALEXAS.

CLEOPATRA Give me some music—music, moody food
Of us that trade in love.

ALL The music, ho!

Enter MARDIAN, *the eunuch.*

CLEOPATRA Let it alone. Let's to billiards. Come, Charmian.

CHARMIAN My arm is sore. Best play with Mardian.

CLEOPATRA As well a woman with an eunuch played
As with a woman. Come, you'll play with me, sir?

MARDIAN As well as I can, madam.

CLEOPATRA And when good will is showed, though't come too short,
The actor may plead pardon. I'll none now.
Give me mine angle; we'll to the river. There,
My music playing far off, I will betray
Tawny-finned fishes. My bended hook shall pierce
Their slimy jaws, and as I draw them up
I'll think them every one an Antony,
And say "Ah, ha! You're caught."

CHARMIAN 'Twas merry when
You wagered on your angling; when your diver
Did hang a salt fish on his hook, which he
With fervency drew up.

CLEOPATRA That time?—O times!—
I laughed him out of patience; and that night
I laughed him into patience, and next morn,

Ere the ninth hour, I drunk him to his bed,
Then put my tires and mantles on him, whilst
I wore his sword Philippan.

Enter MESSENGER.

O! from Italy!
Ram thou thy fruitful tidings in mine ears,
That long time have been barren.

MESSENGER — Madam, madam—

CLEOPATRA — Antony's dead! If thou say so, villain,
Thou kill'st thy mistress. But well and free,
If thou so yield him, there is gold, and here
My bluest veins to kiss, a hand that kings
Have lipped, and trembled kissing.

MESSENGER — First, madam, he's well.

CLEOPATRA — Why, there's more gold.
But sirrah, mark, we use
To say the dead are well. Bring it to that,
The gold I give thee will I melt and pour
Down thy ill-uttering throat.

MESSENGER — Good madam, hear me.

CLEOPATRA — Well, go to, I will.
But there's no goodness in thy face if Antony
Be free and healthful. So tart a favour
To trumpet such good tidings! If not well,
Thou shouldst come like a Fury crowned with snakes,
Not like a formal man.

MESSENGER — Will't please you hear me?

CLEOPATRA — I have a mind to strike thee ere thou speak'st.
Yet if thou say Antony lives, is well,
Or friends with Caesar, or not captive to him,
I'll set thee in a shower of gold and hail
Rich pearls upon thee.

MESSENGER — Madam, he's well.

CLEOPATRA — Well said.

MESSENGER — And friends with Caesar.

CLEOPATRA — Th' art an honest man.

MESSENGER Caesar and he are greater friends than ever.

CLEOPATRA Make thee a fortune from me.

MESSENGER But yet, madam—

CLEOPATRA I do not like "But yet", it does allay
The good precedence. Fie upon "But yet"!
"But yet" is as a gaoler to bring forth
Some monstrous malefactor. Prithee, friend,
Pour out the pack of matter to mine ear,
The good and bad together: he's friends with Caesar,
In state of health, thou say'st; and, thou say'st, free.

MESSENGER Free, madam? No. I made no such report.
He's bound unto Octavia.

CLEOPATRA For what good turn?

MESSENGER For the best turn i' th' bed.

CLEOPATRA I am pale, Charmian.

MESSENGER Madam, he's married to Octavia.

CLEOPATRA The most infectious pestilence upon thee!

[*Strikes him down.*]

MESSENGER Good madam, patience.

CLEOPATRA.

What say you?

[*Strikes him again.*]

Hence, horrible villain, or I'll spurn thine eyes
Like balls before me! I'll unhair thy head!

[*She hales him up and down.*]

Thou shalt be whipped with wire and stewed in brine,
Smarting in ling'ring pickle.

MESSENGER Gracious madam,
I that do bring the news made not the match.

CLEOPATRA Say 'tis not so, a province I will give thee,
And make thy fortunes proud. The blow thou hadst

Shall make thy peace for moving me to rage,
And I will boot thee with what gift beside
Thy modesty can beg.

MESSENGER He's married, madam.

CLEOPATRA Rogue, thou hast lived too long.

[*Draws a knife.*]

MESSENGER Nay then I'll run.
What mean you, madam? I have made no fault.

[*Exit.*]

CHARMIAN Good madam, keep yourself within yourself.
The man is innocent.

CLEOPATRA Some innocents 'scape not the thunderbolt.
Melt Egypt into Nile, and kindly creatures
Turn all to serpents! Call the slave again.
Though I am mad, I will not bite him. Call!

CHARMIAN He is afeard to come.

CLEOPATRA I will not hurt him.

[*Exit* CHARMIAN.]

These hands do lack nobility that they strike
A meaner than myself, since I myself
Have given myself the cause.

Enter the MESSENGER *again with* CHARMIAN.

Come hither, sir.
Though it be honest, it is never good
To bring bad news. Give to a gracious message
An host of tongues, but let ill tidings tell
Themselves when they be felt.

MESSENGER I have done my duty.

CLEOPATRA Is he married?
I cannot hate thee worser than I do
If thou again say "Yes."

MESSENGER He's married, madam.

CLEOPATRA The gods confound thee! Dost thou hold there still!

MESSENGER Should I lie, madam?

CLEOPATRA O, I would thou didst,
So half my Egypt were submerged and made
A cistern for scaled snakes! Go, get thee hence.
Hadst thou Narcissus in thy face, to me
Thou wouldst appear most ugly. He is married?

MESSENGER I crave your highness' pardon.

CLEOPATRA He is married?

MESSENGER Take no offence that I would not offend you.
To punish me for what you make me do
Seems much unequal. He's married to Octavia.

CLEOPATRA O, that his fault should make a knave of thee
That art not what thou'rt sure of! Get thee hence!
The merchandise which thou hast brought from Rome
Are all too dear for me. Lie they upon thy hand,
And be undone by 'em!

[*Exit* MESSENGER.]

CHARMIAN Good your highness, patience.

CLEOPATRA In praising Antony I have dispraised Caesar.

CHARMIAN Many times, madam.

CLEOPATRA I am paid for't now.
Lead me from hence;
I faint. O Iras, Charmian! 'Tis no matter.
Go to the fellow, good Alexas, bid him
Report the feature of Octavia, her years,
Her inclination; let him not leave out
The colour of her hair. Bring me word quickly.

[*Exit* ALEXAS.]

Let him for ever go—let him not, Charmian.
Though he be painted one way like a Gorgon,
The other way 's a Mars. [*To Mardian*] Bid you Alexas
Bring me word how tall she is. Pity me, Charmian,
But do not speak to me. Lead me to my chamber.

[*Exeunt.*]

SCENE-VI — Near Misenum

Flourish. Enter POMPEY *and* MENAS *at one door, with drum and trumpet; at another,* CAESAR, LEPIDUS, ANTONY, ENOBARBUS, MAECENAS, AGRIPPA, *with* SOLDIERS *marching.*

POMPEY
Your hostages I have, so have you mine,
And we shall talk before we fight.

CAESAR
Most meet
That first we come to words, and therefore have we
Our written purposes before us sent,
Which if thou hast considered, let us know
If 'twill tie up thy discontented sword
And carry back to Sicily much tall youth
That else must perish here.

POMPEY
To you all three,
The senators alone of this great world,
Chief factors for the gods: I do not know
Wherefore my father should revengers want,
Having a son and friends, since Julius Caesar,
Who at Philippi the good Brutus ghosted,
There saw you labouring for him. What was't
That moved pale Cassius to conspire? And what
Made the all-honoured, honest Roman, Brutus,
With the armed rest, courtiers of beauteous freedom,
To drench the Capitol, but that they would
Have one man but a man? And that is it
Hath made me rig my navy, at whose burden
The angered ocean foams, with which I meant
To scourge th' ingratitude that despiteful Rome
Cast on my noble father.

CAESAR
Take your time.

ANTONY — Thou canst not fear us, Pompey, with thy sails.
We'll speak with thee at sea. At land thou know'st
How much we do o'ercount thee.

POMPEY — At land indeed
Thou dost o'ercount me of my father's house;
But since the cuckoo builds not for himself,
Remain in't as thou mayst.

LEPIDUS. — Be pleased to tell us—
For this is from the present—how you take
The offers we have sent you.

CAESAR — There's the point.

ANTONY — Which do not be entreated to, but weigh
What it is worth embraced.

CAESAR — And what may follow
To try a larger fortune.

POMPEY — You have made me offer
Of Sicily, Sardinia; and I must
Rid all the sea of pirates; then to send
Measures of wheat to Rome. This 'greed upon,
To part with unhacked edges and bear back
Our targes undinted.

CAESAR, ANTONY, and LEPIDUS — That's our offer.

POMPEY — Know, then,
I came before you here a man prepared
To take this offer. But Mark Antony
Put me to some impatience. Though I lose
The praise of it by telling, you must know
When Caesar and your brother were at blows,
Your mother came to Sicily and did find
Her welcome friendly.

ANTONY — I have heard it, Pompey,
And am well studied for a liberal thanks
Which I do owe you.

POMPEY — Let me have your hand.
I did not think, sir, to have met you here.

ANTONY The beds i' th' East are soft; and thanks to you,
That called me timelier than my purpose hither,
For I have gained by 't.

CAESAR Since I saw you last,
There is a change upon you.

POMPEY Well, I know not
What counts harsh Fortune casts upon my face,
But in my bosom shall she never come
To make my heart her vassal.

LEPIDUS Well met here.

POMPEY I hope so, Lepidus. Thus we are agreed.
I crave our composition may be written
And sealed between us.

CAESAR That's the next to do.

POMPEY We'll feast each other ere we part, and let's
Draw lots who shall begin.

ANTONY That will I, Pompey.

POMPEY No, Antony, take the lot.
But, first or last, your fine Egyptian cookery
Shall have the fame. I have heard that Julius
Caesar
Grew fat with feasting there.

ANTONY You have heard much.

POMPEY I have fair meanings, sir.

ANTONY And fair words to them.

POMPEY Then so much have I heard.
And I have heard Apollodorus carried—

ENOBARBUS No more of that. He did so.

POMPEY What, I pray you?

ENOBARBUS A certain queen to Caesar in a mattress.

POMPEY I know thee now. How far'st thou, soldier?

ENOBARBUS Well;
And well am like to do, for I perceive
Four feasts are toward.

POMPEY Let me shake thy hand.
I never hated thee. I have seen thee fight
When I have envied thy behaviour.

ENOBARBUS Sir,
I never loved you much, but I ha' praised ye
When you have well deserved ten times as much
As I have said you did.

POMPEY Enjoy thy plainness;
It nothing ill becomes thee.
Aboard my galley I invite you all.
Will you lead, lords?

CAESAR, ANTONY, and LEPIDUS Show's the way, sir.

POMPEY Come.

[*Exeunt all but* ENOBARBUS *and* MENAS.]

MENAS [*Aside*.] Thy father, Pompey, would ne'er have made this treaty.—
You and I have known, sir.

ENOBARBUS At sea, I think.

MENAS We have, sir.

ENOBARBUS You have done well by water.

MENAS And you by land.

ENOBARBUS I will praise any man that will praise me, though it cannot be denied what I have done by land.

MENAS Nor what I have done by water.

ENOBARBUS Yes, something you can deny for your own safety: you have been a great thief by sea.

MENAS And you by land.

ENOBARBUS There I deny my land service. But give me your hand, Menas. If our eyes had authority, here they might take two thieves kissing.

MENAS All men's faces are true, whatsome'er their hands are.

ENOBARBUS But there is never a fair woman has a true face.

MENAS No slander. They steal hearts.

ENOBARBUS We came hither to fight with you.

MENAS For my part, I am sorry it is turned to a drinking. Pompey doth this day laugh away his fortune.

ENOBARBUS If he do, sure he cannot weep 't back again.

MENAS You have said, sir. We looked not for Mark Antony here. Pray you, is he married to Cleopatra?

ENOBARBUS Caesar's sister is called Octavia.

MENAS True, sir. She was the wife of Caius Marcellus.

ENOBARBUS But she is now the wife of Marcus Antonius.

MENAS Pray you, sir?

ENOBARBUS 'Tis true.

MENAS Then is Caesar and he for ever knit together.

ENOBARBUS If I were bound to divine of this unity, I would not prophesy so.

MENAS I think the policy of that purpose made more in the marriage than the love of the parties.

ENOBARBUS I think so too. But you shall find the band that seems to tie their friendship together will be the very strangler of their amity. Octavia is of a holy, cold, and still conversation.

MENAS Who would not have his wife so?

ENOBARBUS Not he that himself is not so; which is Mark Antony. He will to his Egyptian dish again. Then shall the sighs of Octavia blow the fire up in Caesar, and, as I said before, that which is the strength of their amity shall prove the immediate author of their variance. Antony will use his affection where it is. He married but his occasion here.

MENAS And thus it may be. Come, sir, will you aboard? I have a health for you.

ENOBARBUS I shall take it, sir. We have used our throats in Egypt.

MENAS Come, let's away.

[*Exeunt.*]

SCENE-VII — On board Pompey's Galley, lying near Misenum

Music. Enter two or three SERVANTS *with a banquet.*

FIRST SERVANT Here they'll be, man. Some o' their plants are ill-rooted already; the least wind i' th' world will blow them down.

SECOND SERVANT Lepidus is high-coloured.

FIRST SERVANT They have made him drink alms-drink.

SECOND SERVANT As they pinch one another by the disposition, he cries out "no more", reconciles them to his entreaty and himself to th' drink.

FIRST SERVANT But it raises the greater war between him and his discretion.

SECOND SERVANT Why, this it is to have a name in great men's fellowship. I had as lief have a reed that will do me no service as a partisan I could not heave.

FIRST SERVANT To be called into a huge sphere, and not to be seen to move in 't, are the holes where eyes should be, which pitifully disaster the cheeks.

A sennet sounded. Enter CAESAR, ANTONY, POMPEY, LEPIDUS, AGRIPPA, MAECENAS, ENOBARBUS, MENAS *with other Captains.*

ANTONY [*To Caesar.*] Thus do they, sir: they take the flow o' th' Nile
By certain scales i' th' pyramid; they know
By th' height, the lowness, or the mean, if dearth
Or foison follow. The higher Nilus swells,
The more it promises. As it ebbs, the seedsman
Upon the slime and ooze scatters his grain,
And shortly comes to harvest.

LEPIDUS You've strange serpents there?

ANTONY Ay, Lepidus.

LEPIDUS Your serpent of Egypt is bred now of your mud by the operation of your sun; so is your crocodile.

ANTONY They are so.

POMPEY Sit, and some wine! A health to Lepidus!

LEPIDUS I am not so well as I should be, but I'll ne'er out.

ENOBARBUS Not till you have slept. I fear me you'll be in till then.

LEPIDUS Nay, certainly, I have heard the Ptolemies' pyramises are very goodly things. Without contradiction I have heard that.

MENAS [*Aside to Pompey.*] Pompey, a word.

POMPEY [*Aside to Menas.*] Say in mine ear what is 't?

MENAS [*Whispers in 's ear.*] Forsake thy seat, I do beseech thee, captain,
And hear me speak a word.

POMPEY [*Aside to Menas.*] Forbear me till anon.—
This wine for Lepidus!

LEPIDUS What manner o' thing is your crocodile?

ANTONY It is shaped, sir, like itself, and it is as broad as it hath breadth. It is just so high as it is, and moves with it own organs. It lives by that which nourisheth it, and the elements once out of it, it transmigrates.

LEPIDUS What colour is it of?

ANTONY Of its own colour too.

LEPIDUS 'Tis a strange serpent.

ANTONY. 'Tis so, and the tears of it are wet.

CAESAR Will this description satisfy him?

ANTONY With the health that Pompey gives him, else he is a very epicure.

POMPEY [*Aside to Menas.*] Go hang, sir, hang! Tell me of that? Away!
Do as I bid you.—Where's this cup I called for?

MENAS [*Aside to Pompey.*] If for the sake of merit thou wilt hear me,
Rise from thy stool.

POMPEY [*Aside to Menas.*] I think thou'rt mad.

[*Rises and walks aside.*]

The matter?

MENAS I have ever held my cap off to thy fortunes.

POMPEY Thou hast served me with much faith. What's else to say?—
Be jolly, lords.

ANTONY These quicksands, Lepidus,
Keep off them, for you sink.

MENAS Wilt thou be lord of all the world?

POMPEY What sayst thou?

MENAS Wilt thou be lord of the whole world?
That's twice.

POMPEY How should that be?

MENAS But entertain it,
And though you think me poor, I am the man
Will give thee all the world.

POMPEY Hast thou drunk well?

MENAS No, Pompey, I have kept me from the cup.
Thou art, if thou dar'st be, the earthly Jove.
Whate'er the ocean pales or sky inclips
Is thine, if thou wilt have't.

POMPEY Show me which way.

MENAS These three world-sharers, these competitors,
Are in thy vessel. Let me cut the cable,
And when we are put off, fall to their throats.
All then is thine.

POMPEY Ah, this thou shouldst have done
And not have spoke on 't! In me 'tis villainy;
In thee 't had been good service. Thou must know
'Tis not my profit that does lead mine honour;
Mine honour it. Repent that e'er thy tongue

Hath so betray'd thine act. Being done unknown,
I should have found it afterwards well done,
But must condemn it now. Desist, and drink.

MENAS — [*Aside.*] For this,
I'll never follow thy palled fortunes more.
Who seeks, and will not take when once 'tis offered,
Shall never find it more.

POMPEY — This health to Lepidus!

ANTONY — Bear him ashore. I'll pledge it for him, Pompey.

ENOBARBUS — Here's to thee, Menas!

MENAS — Enobarbus, welcome!

POMPEY — Fill till the cup be hid.

ENOBARBUS — There's a strong fellow, Menas.

[*Pointing to the servant who carries off* LEPIDUS.]

MENAS — Why?

ENOBARBUS — 'A bears the third part of the world, man. Seest not?

MENAS — The third part, then, is drunk. Would it were all,
That it might go on wheels!

ENOBARBUS — Drink thou. Increase the reels.

MENAS — Come.

POMPEY — This is not yet an Alexandrian feast.

ANTONY — It ripens towards it. Strike the vessels, ho!
Here is to Caesar!

CAESAR — I could well forbear't.
It's monstrous labour when I wash my brain
And it grows fouler.

ANTONY — Be a child o' the time.

CAESAR — Possess it, I'll make answer.
But I had rather fast from all, four days,
Than drink so much in one.

ENOBARBUS — [*To Antony.*] Ha, my brave emperor,
Shall we dance now the Egyptian Bacchanals
And celebrate our drink?

POMPEY Let's ha't, good soldier.

ANTONY Come, let's all take hands
Till that the conquering wine hath steeped our sense
In soft and delicate Lethe.

ENOBARBUS All take hands.
Make battery to our ears with the loud music,
The while I'll place you; then the boy shall sing.
The holding every man shall beat as loud
As his strong sides can volley.

Music plays. ENOBARBUS *places them hand in hand.*

THE SONG Come, thou monarch of the vine,
Plumpy Bacchus with pink eyne!
In thy vats our cares be drowned,
With thy grapes our hairs be crowned.
Cup us till the world go round,
Cup us till the world go round!

CAESAR What would you more? Pompey, good night.
Good brother,
Let me request you off. Our graver business
Frowns at this levity.—Gentle lords, let's part.
You see we have burnt our cheeks. Strong Enobarb
Is weaker than the wine, and mine own tongue
Splits what it speaks. The wild disguise hath almost
Anticked us all. What needs more words. Good night.
Good Antony, your hand.

POMPEY I'll try you on the shore.

ANTONY And shall, sir. Give's your hand.

POMPEY O Antony,
You have my father's house.
But, what? We are friends. Come, down into the boat.

ENOBARBUS Take heed you fall not.

[*Exeunt* POMPEY, CAESAR, ANTONY *and* ATTENDANTS.]

Menas, I'll not on shore.

MENAS — No, to my cabin. These drums, these trumpets, flutes! What!
Let Neptune hear we bid a loud farewell
To these great fellows. Sound and be hanged, sound out!

[*Sound a flourish with drums.*]

ENOBARBUS — Hoo, says 'a! There's my cap!

MENAS — Hoo! Noble captain, come.

[*Exeunt.*]

ACT-III
SCENE-I — A plain in Syria

Enter VENTIDIUS *as it were in triumph, with* SILIUS *and other Romans, Officers and Soldiers; the dead body of* PACORUS *borne before him.*

VENTIDIUS
Now, darting Parthia, art thou struck, and now
Pleased Fortune does of Marcus Crassus' death
Make me revenger. Bear the king's son's body
Before our army. Thy Pacorus, Orodes,
Pays this for Marcus Crassus.

SILIUS
Noble Ventidius,
Whilst yet with Parthian blood thy sword is warm,
The fugitive Parthians follow. Spur through Media,
Mesopotamia, and the shelters whither
The routed fly. So thy grand captain Antony
Shall set thee on triumphant chariots, and
Put garlands on thy head.

VENTIDIUS
O Silius, Silius,
I have done enough. A lower place, note well,
May make too great an act. For learn this, Silius:
Better to leave undone than by our deed
Acquire too high a fame when him we serve's away.
Caesar and Antony have ever won
More in their officer, than person. Sossius,
One of my place in Syria, his lieutenant,
For quick accumulation of renown,
Which he achieved by th' minute, lost his favour.
Who does i' th' wars more than his captain can

Becomes his captain's captain; and ambition,
The soldier's virtue, rather makes choice of loss
Than gain which darkens him.
I could do more to do Antonius good,
But 'twould offend him, and in his offence
Should my performance perish.

SILIUS
Thou hast, Ventidius, that
Without the which a soldier and his sword
Grants scarce distinction. Thou wilt write to Antony?

VENTIDIUS
I'll humbly signify what in his name,
That magical word of war, we have effected;
How, with his banners, and his well-paid ranks,
The ne'er-yet-beaten horse of Parthia
We have jaded out o' th' field.

SILIUS
Where is he now?

VENTIDIUS
He purposeth to Athens, whither, with what haste
The weight we must convey with 's will permit,
We shall appear before him.—On there, pass along!

[*Exeunt.*]

SCENE-II — Rome. An Ante-chamber in Caesar's house

Enter AGRIPPA *at one door,* ENOBARBUS *at another.*

AGRIPPA What, are the brothers parted?

ENOBARBUS They have dispatched with Pompey; he is gone.
The other three are sealing. Octavia weeps
To part from Rome. Caesar is sad, and Lepidus,
Since Pompey's feast, as Menas says, is troubled
With the greensickness.

AGRIPPA 'Tis a noble Lepidus.

ENOBARBUS A very fine one. O, how he loves Caesar!

AGRIPPA Nay, but how dearly he adores Mark Antony!

ENOBARBUS Caesar? Why he's the Jupiter of men.

AGRIPPA What's Antony? The god of Jupiter.

ENOBARBUS Spake you of Caesar? How, the nonpareil!

AGRIPPA O, Antony! O thou Arabian bird!

ENOBARBUS Would you praise Caesar, say "Caesar". Go no further.

AGRIPPA Indeed, he plied them both with excellent praises.

ENOBARBUS But he loves Caesar best, yet he loves Antony.
Hoo! Hearts, tongues, figures, scribes, bards, poets, cannot
Think, speak, cast, write, sing, number—hoo!—
His love to Antony. But as for Caesar,
Kneel down, kneel down, and wonder.

AGRIPPA Both he loves.

ENOBARBUS They are his shards, and he their beetle.

[*Trumpets within.*]

So,
This is to horse. Adieu, noble Agrippa.

AGRIPPA Good fortune, worthy soldier, and farewell.

Enter CAESAR, ANTONY, LEPIDUS *and* OCTAVIA.

ANTONY No further, sir.

CAESAR You take from me a great part of myself.
Use me well in't. Sister, prove such a wife
As my thoughts make thee, and as my farthest bond
Shall pass on thy approof. Most noble Antony,
Let not the piece of virtue which is set
Betwixt us, as the cement of our love
To keep it builded, be the ram to batter
The fortress of it. For better might we
Have loved without this mean, if on both parts
This be not cherished.

ANTONY Make me not offended
In your distrust.

CAESAR I have said.

ANTONY You shall not find,
Though you be therein curious, the least cause
For what you seem to fear. So the gods keep you,
And make the hearts of Romans serve your ends.
We will here part.

CAESAR Farewell, my dearest sister, fare thee well.
The elements be kind to thee, and make
Thy spirits all of comfort! Fare thee well.

OCTAVIA My noble brother!

ANTONY The April's in her eyes. It is love's spring,
And these the showers to bring it on.—Be cheerful.

OCTAVIA Sir, look well to my husband's house, and—

CAESAR What, Octavia?

OCTAVIA I'll tell you in your ear.

ANTONY Her tongue will not obey her heart, nor can
Her heart inform her tongue—the swan's-down feather,
That stands upon the swell at the full of tide,
And neither way inclines.

ENOBARBUS [*Aside to Agrippa.*] Will Caesar weep?

AGRIPPA [*Aside to Enobarbus.*] He has a cloud in 's face.

ENOBARBUS [*Aside to Agrippa.*] He were the worse for that were he a horse;
So is he, being a man.

AGRIPPA [*Aside to Enobarbus.*] Why, Enobarbus,
When Antony found Julius Caesar dead,
He cried almost to roaring, and he wept
When at Philippi he found Brutus slain.

ENOBARBUS [*Aside to Agrippa.*] That year, indeed, he was troubled with a rheum;
What willingly he did confound he wailed,
Believe 't, till I weep too.

CAESAR No, sweet Octavia,
You shall hear from me still. The time shall not
Outgo my thinking on you.

ANTONY Come, sir, come,
I'll wrestle with you in my strength of love.
Look, here I have you, thus I let you go,
And give you to the gods.

CAESAR Adieu, be happy!

LEPIDUS Let all the number of the stars give light
To thy fair way!

CAESAR Farewell, farewell!

[*Kisses* OCTAVIA.]

ANTONY Farewell!

[*Trumpets sound. Exeunt.*]

SCENE-III — Alexandria. A Room in the Palace

Enter CLEOPATRA, CHARMIAN, IRAS *and* ALEXAS.

CLEOPATRA Where is the fellow?

ALEXAS Half afeared to come.

CLEOPATRA Go to, go to.

Enter a MESSENGER *as before.*

Come hither, sir.

ALEXAS Good majesty,
Herod of Jewry dare not look upon you
But when you are well pleased.

CLEOPATRA That Herod's head
I'll have! But how, when Antony is gone,
Through whom I might command it?—Come thou near.

MESSENGER Most gracious majesty!

CLEOPATRA Didst thou behold Octavia?

MESSENGER Ay, dread queen.

CLEOPATRA Where?

MESSENGER Madam, in Rome
I looked her in the face, and saw her led
Between her brother and Mark Antony.

CLEOPATRA Is she as tall as me?

MESSENGER She is not, madam.

CLEOPATRA Didst hear her speak? Is she shrill-tongued or low?

MESSENGER Madam, I heard her speak. She is low-voiced.

CLEOPATRA That's not so good. He cannot like her long.

CHARMIAN Like her? O Isis! 'Tis impossible.

CLEOPATRA I think so, Charmian: dull of tongue and dwarfish!
What majesty is in her gait? Remember,
If e'er thou look'dst on majesty.

MESSENGER She creeps.
Her motion and her station are as one.
She shows a body rather than a life,
A statue than a breather.

CLEOPATRA Is this certain?

MESSENGER Or I have no observance.

CHARMIAN Three in Egypt
Cannot make better note.

CLEOPATRA He's very knowing;
I do perceive't. There's nothing in her yet.
The fellow has good judgment.

CHARMIAN Excellent.

CLEOPATRA Guess at her years, I prithee.

MESSENGER Madam,
She was a widow.

CLEOPATRA Widow! Charmian, hark!

MESSENGER And I do think she's thirty.

CLEOPATRA Bear'st thou her face in mind? Is't long or round?

MESSENGER Round even to faultiness.

CLEOPATRA For the most part, too, they are foolish that are so.
Her hair, what colour?

MESSENGER Brown, madam, and her forehead
As low as she would wish it.

CLEOPATRA There's gold for thee.
Thou must not take my former sharpness ill.
I will employ thee back again; I find thee
Most fit for business. Go make thee ready;
Our letters are prepared.

[*Exit* MESSENGER.]

CHARMIAN A proper man.

CLEOPATRA Indeed, he is so. I repent me much
That so I harried him. Why, methinks, by him,
This creature's no such thing.

CHARMIAN Nothing, madam.

CLEOPATRA The man hath seen some majesty, and should know.

CHARMIAN Hath he seen majesty? Isis else defend,
And serving you so long!

CLEOPATRA I have one thing more to ask him yet, good Charmian.
But 'tis no matter; thou shalt bring him to me
Where I will write. All may be well enough.

CHARMIAN I warrant you, madam.

[*Exeunt.*]

SCENE-IV — Athens. A Room in Antony's House

Enter ANTONY *and* OCTAVIA.

ANTONY Nay, nay, Octavia, not only that—
That were excusable, that and thousands more
Of semblable import—but he hath waged
New wars 'gainst Pompey; made his will, and read it
To public ear;
Spoke scantly of me; when perforce he could not
But pay me terms of honour, cold and sickly
He vented them; most narrow measure lent me;
When the best hint was given him, he not took 't,
Or did it from his teeth.

OCTAVIA O, my good lord,
Believe not all, or if you must believe,
Stomach not all. A more unhappy lady,
If this division chance, ne'er stood between,
Praying for both parts.
The good gods will mock me presently
When I shall pray "O, bless my lord and husband!"
Undo that prayer by crying out as loud
"O, bless my brother!" Husband win, win brother,
Prays and destroys the prayer; no midway
'Twixt these extremes at all.

ANTONY Gentle Octavia,
Let your best love draw to that point which seeks
Best to preserve it. If I lose mine honour,
I lose myself; better I were not yours
Than yours so branchless. But, as you requested,
Yourself shall go between's. The meantime, lady,
I'll raise the preparation of a war

Shall stain your brother. Make your soonest haste,
So your desires are yours.

OCTAVIA Thanks to my lord.
The Jove of power make me, most weak, most weak,
Your reconciler! Wars 'twixt you twain would be
As if the world should cleave, and that slain men
Should solder up the rift.

ANTONY When it appears to you where this begins,
Turn your displeasure that way, for our faults
Can never be so equal that your love
Can equally move with them. Provide your going;
Choose your own company, and command what cost
Your heart has mind to.

[*Exeunt.*]

SCENE-V — Athens. Another Room in Antony's House

Enter ENOBARBUS *and* EROS *meeting.*

ENOBARBUS How now, friend Eros?

EROS There's strange news come, sir.

ENOBARBUS What, man?

EROS Caesar and Lepidus have made wars upon Pompey.

ENOBARBUS This is old. What is the success?

EROS Caesar, having made use of him in the wars 'gainst Pompey, presently denied him rivality; would not let him partake in the glory of the action, and, not resting here, accuses him of letters he had formerly wrote to Pompey; upon his own appeal, seizes him. So the poor third is up, till death enlarge his confine.

ENOBARBUS Then, world, thou hast a pair of chaps, no more,
And throw between them all the food thou hast,
They'll grind the one the other. Where's
Antony?

EROS He's walking in the garden, thus, and spurns
The rush that lies before him; cries "Fool
Lepidus!"
And threats the throat of that his officer
That murdered Pompey.

ENOBARBUS Our great navy's rigged.

EROS For Italy and Caesar. More, Domitius:
My lord desires you presently. My news
I might have told hereafter.

ENOBARBUS 'Twill be naught,
But let it be. Bring me to Antony.

EROS Come, sir.

[*Exeunt.*]

SCENE-VI — Rome. A Room in Caesar's House

Enter AGRIPPA, MAECENAS *and* CAESAR.

CAESAR
Contemning Rome, he has done all this, and more
In Alexandria. Here's the manner of 't:
I' th' market-place, on a tribunal silvered,
Cleopatra and himself in chairs of gold
Were publicly enthroned. At the feet sat
Caesarion, whom they call my father's son,
And all the unlawful issue that their lust
Since then hath made between them. Unto her
He gave the stablishment of Egypt; made her
Of lower Syria, Cyprus, Lydia,
Absolute queen.

MAECENAS
This in the public eye?

CAESAR
I' th' common showplace where they exercise.
His sons he there proclaimed the kings of kings:
Great Media, Parthia, and Armenia
He gave to Alexander; to Ptolemy he assigned
Syria, Cilicia, and Phoenicia. She
In th' habiliments of the goddess Isis
That day appeared, and oft before gave audience,
As 'tis reported, so.

MAECENAS
Let Rome be thus informed.

AGRIPPA
Who, queasy with his insolence already,
Will their good thoughts call from him.

CAESAR
The people knows it and have now received
His accusations.

AGRIPPA Who does he accuse?

CAESAR Caesar, and that, having in Sicily
Sextus Pompeius spoiled, we had not rated him
His part o' th' isle. Then does he say he lent me
Some shipping, unrestored. Lastly, he frets
That Lepidus of the triumvirate
Should be deposed and, being, that we detain
All his revenue.

AGRIPPA Sir, this should be answered.

CAESAR 'Tis done already, and messenger gone.
I have told him Lepidus was grown too cruel,
That he his high authority abused,
And did deserve his change. For what I have conquered
I grant him part; but then in his Armenia
And other of his conquered kingdoms, I
Demand the like.

MAECENAS He'll never yield to that.

CAESAR Nor must not then be yielded to in this.

Enter OCTAVIA *with her train.*

OCTAVIA Hail, Caesar, and my lord! Hail, most dear Caesar!

CAESAR That ever I should call thee castaway!

OCTAVIA You have not called me so, nor have you cause.

CAESAR Why have you stolen upon us thus? You come not
Like Caesar's sister. The wife of Antony
Should have an army for an usher, and
The neighs of horse to tell of her approach
Long ere she did appear. The trees by th' way
Should have borne men, and expectation fainted,
Longing for what it had not. Nay, the dust
Should have ascended to the roof of heaven,
Raised by your populous troops. But you are come
A market-maid to Rome, and have prevented

The ostentation of our love, which, left unshown,
Is often left unloved. We should have met you
By sea and land, supplying every stage
With an augmented greeting.

OCTAVIA Good my lord,
To come thus was I not constrained, but did it
On my free will. My lord, Mark Antony,
Hearing that you prepared for war, acquainted
My grieved ear withal, whereon I begged
His pardon for return.

CAESAR Which soon he granted,
Being an abstract 'tween his lust and him.

OCTAVIA Do not say so, my lord.

CAESAR I have eyes upon him,
And his affairs come to me on the wind.
Where is he now?

OCTAVIA My lord, in Athens.

CAESAR No, my most wronged sister. Cleopatra
Hath nodded him to her. He hath given his empire
Up to a whore, who now are levying
The kings o' th' earth for war. He hath assembled
Bocchus, the king of Libya; Archelaus
Of Cappadocia; Philadelphos, king
Of Paphlagonia; the Thracian king, Adallas;
King Manchus of Arabia; King of Pont;
Herod of Jewry; Mithridates, king
Of Comagene; Polemon and Amyntas,
The kings of Mede and Lycaonia,
With a more larger list of sceptres.

OCTAVIA Ay me, most wretched,
That have my heart parted betwixt two friends
That does afflict each other!

CAESAR Welcome hither.
Your letters did withhold our breaking forth
Till we perceived both how you were wrong led

And we in negligent danger. Cheer your heart.
Be you not troubled with the time, which drives
O'er your content these strong necessities,
But let determined things to destiny
Hold unbewailed their way. Welcome to Rome,
Nothing more dear to me. You are abused
Beyond the mark of thought, and the high gods,
To do you justice, make their ministers
Of us and those that love you. Best of comfort,
And ever welcome to us.

AGRIPPA Welcome, lady.

MAECENAS Welcome, dear madam.
Each heart in Rome does love and pity you.
Only th' adulterous Antony, most large
In his abominations, turns you off
And gives his potent regiment to a trull
That noises it against us.

OCTAVIA Is it so, sir?

CAESAR Most certain. Sister, welcome. Pray you
Be ever known to patience. My dear'st sister!

[*Exeunt.*]

SCENE-VII — Antony's Camp near the Promontory of Actium

Enter CLEOPATRA *and* ENOBARBUS.

CLEOPATRA	I will be even with thee, doubt it not.
ENOBARBUS	But why, why, why?
CLEOPATRA	Thou hast forspoke my being in these wars And say'st it is not fit.
ENOBARBUS	Well, is it, is it?
CLEOPATRA	Is 't not denounced against us? Why should not we Be there in person?
ENOBARBUS	Well, I could reply: If we should serve with horse and mares together, The horse were merely lost. The mares would bear A soldier and his horse.
CLEOPATRA	What is't you say?
ENOBARBUS	Your presence needs must puzzle Antony, Take from his heart, take from his brain, from 's time, What should not then be spared. He is already Traduced for levity, and 'tis said in Rome That Photinus, an eunuch, and your maids Manage this war.
CLEOPATRA	Sink Rome, and their tongues rot That speak against us! A charge we bear i' th' war, And, as the president of my kingdom, will

Appear there for a man. Speak not against it.
I will not stay behind.

Enter ANTONY *and* CANIDIUS.

ENOBARBUS Nay, I have done.
Here comes the Emperor.

ANTONY Is it not strange, Canidius,
That from Tarentum and Brundusium
He could so quickly cut the Ionian sea
And take in Toryne?—You have heard on 't, sweet?

CLEOPATRA Celerity is never more admired
Than by the negligent.

ANTONY A good rebuke,
Which might have well becomed the best of men
To taunt at slackness.—Canidius, we
Will fight with him by sea.

CLEOPATRA By sea, what else?

CANIDIUS Why will my lord do so?

ANTONY For that he dares us to 't.

ENOBARBUS So hath my lord dared him to single fight.

CANIDIUS Ay, and to wage this battle at Pharsalia,
Where Caesar fought with Pompey. But these offers,
Which serve not for his vantage, he shakes off,
And so should you.

ENOBARBUS Your ships are not well manned,
Your mariners are muleteers, reapers, people
Engrossed by swift impress. In Caesar's fleet
Are those that often have 'gainst Pompey fought.
Their ships are yare, yours heavy. No disgrace
Shall fall you for refusing him at sea,
Being prepared for land.

ANTONY By sea, by sea.

ENOBARBUS Most worthy sir, you therein throw away

The absolute soldiership you have by land;
Distract your army, which doth most consist
Of war-marked footmen; leave unexecuted
Your own renowned knowledge; quite forgo
The way which promises assurance; and
Give up yourself merely to chance and hazard
From firm security.

ANTONY I'll fight at sea.

CLEOPATRA I have sixty sails, Caesar none better.

ANTONY Our overplus of shipping will we burn,
And with the rest full-manned, from th' head of Actium
Beat th' approaching Caesar. But if we fail,
We then can do 't at land.

Enter a MESSENGER.

Thy business?

MESSENGER The news is true, my lord; he is descried.
Caesar has taken Toryne.

ANTONY Can he be there in person? 'Tis impossible;
Strange that his power should be. Canidius,
Our nineteen legions thou shalt hold by land,
And our twelve thousand horse. We'll to our ship.
Away, my Thetis!

Enter a SOLDIER.

How now, worthy soldier?

SOLDIER O noble emperor, do not fight by sea.
Trust not to rotten planks. Do you misdoubt
This sword and these my wounds? Let th' Egyptians
And the Phoenicians go a-ducking. We
Have used to conquer standing on the earth
And fighting foot to foot.

ANTONY Well, well, away.

[*Exeunt* ANTONY, CLEOPATRA *and* ENOBARBUS.]

SOLDIER By Hercules, I think I am i' th' right.

CANIDIUS — Soldier, thou art. But his whole action grows
Not in the power on 't. So our leader's led,
And we are women's men.

SOLDIER — You keep by land
The legions and the horse whole, do you not?

CANIDIUS — Marcus Octavius, Marcus Justeius,
Publicola, and Caelius are for sea,
But we keep whole by land. This speed of Caesar's
Carries beyond belief.

SOLDIER — While he was yet in Rome,
His power went out in such distractions as
Beguiled all spies.

CANIDIUS — Who's his lieutenant, hear you?

SOLDIER — They say one Taurus.

CANIDIUS — Well I know the man.

Enter a MESSENGER.

MESSENGER — The Emperor calls Canidius.

CANIDIUS — With news the time's with labour, and throes forth
Each minute some.

[*Exeunt.*]

SCENE-VIII — A plain near Actium

Enter CAESAR *with his army and* TAURUS *marching.*

CAESAR	Taurus!
TAURUS	My lord?
CAESAR	Strike not by land; keep whole; provoke not battle Till we have done at sea. Do not exceed The prescript of this scroll. Our fortune lies Upon this jump.

[*Exeunt.*]

SCENE-IX — Another part of the Plain

Enter ANTONY *and* ENOBARBUS.

ANTONY Set we our squadrons on yon side o' th' hill
In eye of Caesar's battle, from which place
We may the number of the ships behold
And so proceed accordingly.

[*Exeunt.*]

SCENE-X — Another part of the Plain

CANIDIUS *marching with his land army one way over the stage, and* TAURUS, *the Lieutenant of* CAESAR, *with his Army, the other way. After their going in, is heard the noise of a sea fight.*

Alarum. Enter ENOBARBUS.

ENOBARBUS
Naught, naught, all naught! I can behold no longer.
Th' Antoniad, the Egyptian admiral,
With all their sixty, fly and turn the rudder.
To see 't mine eyes are blasted.

Enter SCARUS.

SCARUS
Gods and goddesses,
All the whole synod of them!

ENOBARBUS
What's thy passion?

SCARUS
The greater cantle of the world is lost
With very ignorance. We have kissed away
Kingdoms and provinces.

ENOBARBUS
How appears the fight?

SCARUS
On our side like, the tokened pestilence,
Where death is sure. Yon ribaudred nag of Egypt,
Whom leprosy o'ertake, i' th' midst o' th' fight,
When vantage like a pair of twins appeared,
Both as the same—or, rather, ours the elder—
The breeze upon her, like a cow in June,
Hoists sails and flies.

ENOBARBUS
That I beheld.
Mine eyes did sicken at the sight and could not
Endure a further view.

SCARUS She once being loofed,
The noble ruin of her magic, Antony,
Claps on his sea-wing and, like a doting mallard,
Leaving the fight in height, flies after her.
I never saw an action of such shame.
Experience, manhood, honour, ne'er before
Did violate so itself.

ENOBARBUS Alack, alack!

Enter CANIDIUS.

CANIDIUS Our fortune on the sea is out of breath
And sinks most lamentably. Had our general
Been what he knew himself, it had gone well.
O, he has given example for our flight
Most grossly by his own!

ENOBARBUS Ay, are you thereabouts?
Why, then, good night indeed.

CANIDIUS Toward Peloponnesus are they fled.

SCARUS 'Tis easy to't, and there I will attend
What further comes.

CANIDIUS To Caesar will I render
My legions and my horse. Six kings already
Show me the way of yielding.

ENOBARBUS I'll yet follow
The wounded chance of Antony, though my reason
Sits in the wind against me.

[*Exeunt.*]

SCENE-XI — Alexandria. A Room in the Palace

Enter ANTONY *with attendants.*

ANTONY
Hark, the land bids me tread no more upon't.
It is ashamed to bear me. Friends, come hither.
I am so lated in the world that I
Have lost my way for ever. I have a ship
Laden with gold. Take that, divide it. Fly,
And make your peace with Caesar.

ALL
Fly? Not we.

ANTONY
I have fled myself, and have instructed cowards
To run and show their shoulders. Friends, be gone.
I have myself resolved upon a course
Which has no need of you. Be gone.
My treasure's in the harbour. Take it. O,
I followed that I blush to look upon.
My very hairs do mutiny, for the white
Reprove the brown for rashness, and they them
For fear and doting. Friends, be gone. You shall
Have letters from me to some friends that will
Sweep your way for you. Pray you, look not sad,
Nor make replies of loathness. Take the hint
Which my despair proclaims. Let that be left
Which leaves itself. To the sea-side straightway.
I will possess you of that ship and treasure.
Leave me, I pray, a little—pray you, now,
Nay, do so; for indeed I have lost command.
Therefore I pray you. I'll see you by and by.

[*Sits down.*]

Enter CLEOPATRA *led by* CHARMIAN, IRAS *and* EROS.

EROS — Nay, gentle madam, to him! Comfort him.

IRAS — Do, most dear queen.

CHARMIAN — Do! Why, what else?

CLEOPATRA — Let me sit down. O Juno!

ANTONY — No, no, no, no, no.

EROS — See you here, sir?

ANTONY — O, fie, fie, fie!

CHARMIAN — Madam.

IRAS — Madam, O good empress!

EROS — Sir, sir!

ANTONY — Yes, my lord, yes. He at Philippi kept
His sword e'en like a dancer, while I struck
The lean and wrinkled Cassius, and 'twas I
That the mad Brutus ended. He alone
Dealt on lieutenantry, and no practice had
In the brave squares of war. Yet now—no matter.

CLEOPATRA — Ah, stand by.

EROS — The Queen, my lord, the Queen!

IRAS — Go to him, madam; speak to him.
He is unqualitied with very shame.

CLEOPATRA — Well then, sustain me. O!

EROS — Most noble sir, arise. The Queen approaches.
Her head's declined, and death will seize her but
Your comfort makes the rescue.

ANTONY — I have offended reputation,
A most unnoble swerving.

EROS — Sir, the Queen.

ANTONY — O, whither hast thou led me, Egypt? See
How I convey my shame out of thine eyes
By looking back what I have left behind
'Stroyed in dishonour.

CLEOPATRA — O my lord, my lord,
Forgive my fearful sails! I little thought
You would have followed.

ANTONY
Egypt, thou knew'st too well
My heart was to thy rudder tied by th' strings,
And thou shouldst tow me after. O'er my spirit
Thy full supremacy thou knew'st, and that
Thy beck might from the bidding of the gods
Command me.

CLEOPATRA
O, my pardon!

ANTONY
Now I must
To the young man send humble treaties, dodge
And palter in the shifts of lowness, who
With half the bulk o' th' world played as I pleased,
Making and marring fortunes. You did know
How much you were my conqueror, and that
My sword, made weak by my affection, would
Obey it on all cause.

CLEOPATRA
Pardon, pardon!

ANTONY
Fall not a tear, I say; one of them rates
All that is won and lost. Give me a kiss.
Even this repays me.
We sent our schoolmaster. Is he come back?
Love, I am full of lead. Some wine
Within there, and our viands! Fortune knows
We scorn her most when most she offers blows.

[*Exeunt.*]

SCENE-XII — Caesar's camp in Egypt

Enter CAESAR, AGRIPPA, DOLABELLA *with others.*

CAESAR — Let him appear that's come from Antony.
Know you him?

DOLABELLA — Caesar, 'tis his schoolmaster—
An argument that he is plucked, when hither
He sends so poor a pinion of his wing,
Which had superfluous kings for messengers
Not many moons gone by.

Enter AMBASSADOR *from* ANTHONY.

CAESAR — Approach, and speak.

AMBASSADOR — Such as I am, I come from Antony.
I was of late as petty to his ends
As is the morn-dew on the myrtle leaf
To his grand sea.

CAESAR — Be't so. Declare thine office.

AMBASSADOR — Lord of his fortunes he salutes thee, and
Requires to live in Egypt, which not granted,
He lessens his requests, and to thee sues
To let him breathe between the heavens and earth,
A private man in Athens. This for him.
Next, Cleopatra does confess thy greatness,
Submits her to thy might, and of thee craves
The circle of the Ptolemies for her heirs,
Now hazarded to thy grace.

CAESAR — For Antony,
I have no ears to his request. The queen
Of audience nor desire shall fail, so she

From Egypt drive her all-disgraced friend,
Or take his life there. This if she perform,
She shall not sue unheard. So to them both.

AMBASSADOR Fortune pursue thee!

CAESAR Bring him through the bands.

[*Exit* AMBASSADOR, *attended.*]

[*To Thidias.*] To try thy eloquence now 'tis time.
Dispatch.
From Antony win Cleopatra. Promise,
And in our name, what she requires; add more,
From thine invention, offers. Women are not
In their best fortunes strong, but want will
perjure
The ne'er-touch'd vestal. Try thy cunning,
Thidias;
Make thine own edict for thy pains, which we
Will answer as a law.

THIDIAS Caesar, I go.

CAESAR Observe how Antony becomes his flaw,
And what thou think'st his very action speaks
In every power that moves.

THIDIAS Caesar, I shall.

[*Exeunt.*]

SCENE-XIII — Alexandria. A Room in the Palace

Enter CLEOPATRA, ENOBARBUS, CHARMIAN *and* IRAS.

CLEOPATRA What shall we do, Enobarbus?

ENOBARBUS Think, and die.

CLEOPATRA Is Antony or we in fault for this?

ENOBARBUS Antony only, that would make his will
Lord of his reason. What though you fled
From that great face of war, whose several ranges
Frighted each other? Why should he follow?
The itch of his affection should not then
Have nicked his captainship, at such a point,
When half to half the world opposed, he being
The mered question. 'Twas a shame no less
Than was his loss, to course your flying flags
And leave his navy gazing.

CLEOPATRA Prithee, peace.

Enter the AMBASSADOr *with* ANTONY.

ANTONY Is that his answer?

AMBASSADOR Ay, my lord.

ANTONY The Queen shall then have courtesy, so she
Will yield us up.

AMBASSADOR He says so.

ANTONY Let her know't.—
To the boy Caesar send this grizzled head,
And he will fill thy wishes to the brim
With principalities.

CLEOPATRA That head, my lord?

ANTONY — To him again. Tell him he wears the rose
Of youth upon him, from which the world should note
Something particular: his coin, ships, legions,
May be a coward's; whose ministers would prevail
Under the service of a child as soon
As i' th' command of Caesar. I dare him therefore
To lay his gay comparisons apart,
And answer me declined, sword against sword,
Ourselves alone. I'll write it. Follow me.

[Exeunt ANTONY *and* AMBASSADOR.*]*

ENOBARBUS — Yes, like enough high-battled Caesar will
Unstate his happiness, and be staged to th' show
Against a sworder! I see men's judgments are
A parcel of their fortunes, and things outward
Do draw the inward quality after them
To suffer all alike. That he should dream,
Knowing all measures, the full Caesar will
Answer his emptiness! Caesar, thou hast subdued
His judgment too.

Enter a SERVANT.

SERVANT — A messenger from Caesar.

CLEOPATRA — What, no more ceremony? See, my women,
Against the blown rose may they stop their nose
That kneeled unto the buds. Admit him, sir.

[*Exit* SERVANT.]

ENOBARBUS — [*Aside.*] Mine honesty and I begin to square.
The loyalty well held to fools does make
Our faith mere folly. Yet he that can endure
To follow with allegiance a fallen lord
Does conquer him that did his master conquer,
And earns a place i' th' story.

Enter THIDIAS.

CLEOPATRA Caesar's will?

THIDIAS Hear it apart.

CLEOPATRA None but friends. Say boldly.

THIDIAS So haply are they friends to Antony.

ENOBARBUS He needs as many, sir, as Caesar has,
Or needs not us. If Caesar please, our master
Will leap to be his friend. For us, you know
Whose he is we are, and that is Caesar's.

THIDIAS So.—
Thus then, thou most renowned: Caesar entreats
Not to consider in what case thou stand'st
Further than he is Caesar.

CLEOPATRA Go on; right royal.

THIDIAS He knows that you embrace not Antony
As you did love, but as you feared him.

CLEOPATRA O!

THIDIAS The scars upon your honour, therefore, he
Does pity as constrained blemishes,
Not as deserved.

CLEOPATRA He is a god and knows
What is most right. Mine honour was not yielded,
But conquered merely.

ENOBARBUS [*Aside*.] To be sure of that,
I will ask Antony. Sir, sir, thou art so leaky
That we must leave thee to thy sinking, for
Thy dearest quit thee.

[*Exit* ENOBARBUS.]

THIDIAS Shall I say to Caesar
What you require of him? For he partly begs
To be desired to give. It much would please him
That of his fortunes you should make a staff
To lean upon. But it would warm his spirits
To hear from me you had left Antony,
And put yourself under his shroud,
The universal landlord.

CLEOPATRA What's your name?

THIDIAS My name is Thidias.

CLEOPATRA Most kind messenger,
Say to great Caesar this in deputation:
I kiss his conqu'ring hand. Tell him I am prompt
To lay my crown at's feet, and there to kneel.
Tell him, from his all-obeying breath I hear
The doom of Egypt.

THIDIAS 'Tis your noblest course.
Wisdom and fortune combating together,
If that the former dare but what it can,
No chance may shake it. Give me grace to lay
My duty on your hand.

CLEOPATRA Your Caesar's father oft,
When he hath mused of taking kingdoms in,
Bestowed his lips on that unworthy place
As it rained kisses.

Enter ANTONY *and* ENOBARBUS.

ANTONY Favours, by Jove that thunders!
What art thou, fellow?

THIDIAS One that but performs
The bidding of the fullest man and worthiest
To have command obeyed.

ENOBARBUS [*Aside*.] You will be whipped.

ANTONY Approach there.—Ah, you kite!—Now, gods and devils,
Authority melts from me. Of late when I cried "Ho!"
Like boys unto a muss, kings would start forth
And cry "Your will?" Have you no ears? I am Antony yet.

Enter SERVANTS.

Take hence this jack and whip him.

ENOBARBUS 'Tis better playing with a lion's whelp
Than with an old one dying.

ANTONY Moon and stars!
Whip him. Were't twenty of the greatest

tributaries
That do acknowledge Caesar, should I find them
So saucy with the hand of she here—what's her name
Since she was Cleopatra? Whip him, fellows,
Till like a boy you see him cringe his face
And whine aloud for mercy. Take him hence.

THIDIAS Mark Antony—

ANTONY Tug him away. Being whipp'd,
Bring him again. This jack of Caesar's shall
Bear us an errand to him.

[*Exeunt Servants with* THIDIAS.]

You were half blasted ere I knew you. Ha!
Have I my pillow left unpressed in Rome,
Forborne the getting of a lawful race,
And by a gem of women, to be abused
By one that looks on feeders?

CLEOPATRA Good my lord—

ANTONY You have been a boggler ever.
But when we in our viciousness grow hard—
O misery on't!—the wise gods seal our eyes,
In our own filth drop our clear judgments, make us
Adore our errors, laugh at's while we strut
To our confusion.

CLEOPATRA O, is't come to this?

ANTONY I found you as a morsel cold upon
Dead Caesar's trencher; nay, you were a fragment
Of Gneius Pompey's, besides what hotter hours,
Unregistered in vulgar fame, you have
Luxuriously pick'd out. For I am sure,
Though you can guess what temperance should be,
You know not what it is.

CLEOPATRA Wherefore is this?

ANTONY To let a fellow that will take rewards

And say "God quit you!" be familiar with
My playfellow, your hand, this kingly seal
And plighter of high hearts! O that I were
Upon the hill of Basan, to outroar
The horned herd! For I have savage cause,
And to proclaim it civilly were like
A haltered neck which does the hangman thank
For being yare about him.

Enter a SERVANT *with* THIDIAS.

Is he whipped?

SERVANT Soundly, my lord.

ANTONY Cried he? And begged he pardon?

SERVANT He did ask favour.

ANTONY If that thy father live, let him repent
Thou wast not made his daughter; and be thou sorry
To follow Caesar in his triumph, since
Thou hast been whipped for following him. Henceforth
The white hand of a lady fever thee;
Shake thou to look on't. Get thee back to Caesar;
Tell him thy entertainment. Look thou say
He makes me angry with him; for he seems
Proud and disdainful, harping on what I am,
Not what he knew I was. He makes me angry,
And at this time most easy 'tis to do't,
When my good stars that were my former guides
Have empty left their orbs and shot their fires
Into th' abysm of hell. If he mislike
My speech and what is done, tell him he has
Hipparchus, my enfranched bondman, whom
He may at pleasure whip, or hang, or torture,
As he shall like, to quit me. Urge it thou.
Hence with thy stripes, be gone.

[*Exit* THIDIAS.]

CLEOPATRA Have you done yet?

ANTONY	Alack, our terrene moon is now eclipsed, And it portends alone the fall of Antony.
CLEOPATRA	I must stay his time.
ANTONY	To flatter Caesar, would you mingle eyes With one that ties his points?
CLEOPATRA	Not know me yet?
ANTONY	Cold-hearted toward me?
CLEOPATRA	Ah, dear, if I be so, From my cold heart let heaven engender hail And poison it in the source, and the first stone Drop in my neck; as it determines, so Dissolve my life! The next Caesarion smite, Till, by degrees the memory of my womb, Together with my brave Egyptians all, By the discandying of this pelleted storm, Lie graveless, till the flies and gnats of Nile Have buried them for prey!
ANTONY	I am satisfied. Caesar sits down in Alexandria, where I will oppose his fate. Our force by land Hath nobly held; our severed navy too Have knit again, and fleet, threat'ning most sea-like. Where hast thou been, my heart? Dost thou hear, lady? If from the field I shall return once more To kiss these lips, I will appear in blood. I and my sword will earn our chronicle. There's hope in't yet.
CLEOPATRA	That's my brave lord!
ANTONY	I will be treble-sinewed, hearted, breathed, And fight maliciously. For when mine hours Were nice and lucky, men did ransom lives Of me for jests. But now I'll set my teeth And send to darkness all that stop me. Come, Let's have one other gaudy night. Call to me All my sad captains. Fill our bowls once more Let's mock the midnight bell.

CLEOPATRA — It is my birthday.
I had thought t'have held it poor, but since my lord
Is Antony again, I will be Cleopatra.

ANTONY — We will yet do well.

CLEOPATRA — Call all his noble captains to my lord.

ANTONY — Do so; we'll speak to them; and tonight I'll force
The wine peep through their scars. Come on, my queen,
There's sap in't yet. The next time I do fight
I'll make Death love me, for I will contend
Even with his pestilent scythe.

[*Exeunt all but* ENOBARBUS.]

ENOBARBUS — Now he'll outstare the lightning. To be furious
Is to be frighted out of fear, and in that mood
The dove will peck the estridge; and I see still
A diminution in our captain's brain
Restores his heart. When valour preys on reason,
It eats the sword it fights with. I will seek
Some way to leave him.

[*Exit.*]

ACT-IV
SCENE-I — Caesar's Camp at Alexandria

Enter CAESAR, AGRIPPA, *and* MAECENAS, *with his army.* CAESAR *reading a letter.*

CAESAR

He calls me boy, and chides as he had power
To beat me out of Egypt. My messenger
He hath whipped with rods; dares me to personal combat,
Caesar to Antony. Let the old ruffian know
I have many other ways to die; meantime
Laugh at his challenge.

MAECENAS

Caesar must think,
When one so great begins to rage, he's hunted
Even to falling. Give him no breath, but now
Make boot of his distraction. Never anger
Made good guard for itself.

CAESAR

Let our best heads
Know that tomorrow the last of many battles
We mean to fight. Within our files there are,
Of those that served Mark Antony but late,
Enough to fetch him in. See it done,
And feast the army; we have store to do't,
And they have earned the waste. Poor Antony!

[*Exeunt.*]

SCENE-II — Alexandria. A Room in the Palace

Enter ANTONY, CLEOPATRA, ENOBARBUS, CHARMIAN, IRAS, ALEXAS *with others.*

ANTONY He will not fight with me, Domitius?

ENOBARBUS No.

ANTONY Why should he not?

ENOBARBUS He thinks, being twenty times of better fortune,
He is twenty men to one.

ANTONY Tomorrow, soldier,
By sea and land I'll fight. Or I will live,
Or bathe my dying honour in the blood
Shall make it live again. Woo't thou fight well?

ENOBARBUS I'll strike, and cry "Take all."

ANTONY Well said. Come on.
Call forth my household servants. Let's tonight
Be bounteous at our meal.—

Enter SERVANTS.

Give me thy hand.
Thou has been rightly honest; so hast thou,
Thou, and thou, and thou. You have served me well,
And kings have been your fellows.

CLEOPATRA [*Aside to Enobarbus.*] What means this?

ENOBARBUS [*Aside to Cleopatra.*] 'Tis one of those odd tricks which sorrow shoots
Out of the mind.

ANTONY And thou art honest too.
I wish I could be made so many men,
And all of you clapped up together in

An Antony, that I might do you service
So good as you have done.

ALL THE SERVANTS The gods forbid!

ANTONY Well, my good fellows, wait on me tonight.
Scant not my cups, and make as much of me
As when mine empire was your fellow too
And suffered my command.

CLEOPATRA [*Aside to Enobarbus.*] What does he mean?

ENOBARBUS [*Aside to Cleopatra.*] To make his followers weep.

ANTONY Tend me tonight;
May be it is the period of your duty.
Haply you shall not see me more, or if,
A mangled shadow. Perchance tomorrow
You'll serve another master. I look on you
As one that takes his leave. Mine honest friends,
I turn you not away, but, like a master
Married to your good service, stay till death.
Tend me tonight two hours, I ask no more,
And the gods yield you for't!

ENOBARBUS What mean you, sir,
To give them this discomfort? Look, they weep,
And I, an ass, am onion-eyed. For shame,
Transform us not to women.

ANTONY Ho, ho, ho!
Now the witch take me if I meant it thus!
Grace grow where those drops fall! My hearty friends,
You take me in too dolorous a sense,
For I spake to you for your comfort, did desire you
To burn this night with torches. Know, my hearts,
I hope well of tomorrow, and will lead you
Where rather I'll expect victorious life
Than death and honour. Let's to supper, come,
And drown consideration.

[*Exeunt.*]

SCENE-III — Alexandria. Before the Palace

Enter a Company of SOLDIERS.

FIRST SOLDIER Brother, good night. Tomorrow is the day.

SECOND SOLDIER It will determine one way. Fare you well.
Heard you of nothing strange about the streets?

FIRST SOLDIER Nothing. What news?

SECOND SOLDIER Belike 'tis but a rumour. Good night to you.

FIRST SOLDIER Well, sir, good night.

Enter two other SOLDIERS.

SECOND SOLDIER Soldiers, have careful watch.

THIRD SOLDIER And you. Good night, good night.

[*They place themselves in every corner of the stage.*]

SECOND SOLDIER Here we. And if tomorrow
Our navy thrive, I have an absolute hope
Our landmen will stand up.

FIRST SOLDIER 'Tis a brave army, and full of purpose.

[*Music of the hautboys under the stage.*]

SECOND SOLDIER Peace, what noise?

FIRST SOLDIER List, list!

SECOND SOLDIER Hark!

FIRST SOLDIER Music i' th' air.

THIRD SOLDIER Under the earth.

FOURTH SOLDIER It signs well, does it not?

THIRD SOLDIER No.

FIRST SOLDIER Peace, I say! What should this mean?

SECOND SOLDIER 'Tis the god Hercules, whom Antony loved,
Now leaves him.

FIRST SOLDIER Walk. Let's see if other watchmen
Do hear what we do.

[*They advance to another post.*]

SECOND SOLDIER How now, masters!

ALL How now! How now! Do you hear this?

FIRST SOLDIER Ay. Is't not strange?

THIRD SOLDIER Do you hear, masters? Do you hear?

FIRST SOLDIER Follow the noise so far as we have quarter.
Let's see how it will give off.

ALL Content. 'Tis strange.

[*Exeunt.*]

SCENE-IV — Alexandria. A Room in the Palace

Enter ANTONY *and* CLEOPATRA *with others.*

ANTONY — Eros! Mine armour, Eros!

CLEOPATRA — Sleep a little.

ANTONY — No, my chuck.—Eros! Come, mine armour, Eros!

Enter EROS *with* ARMOUR.

Come, good fellow, put thine iron on.
If fortune be not ours today, it is
Because we brave her. Come.

CLEOPATRA — Nay, I'll help too.
What's this for?

ANTONY — Ah, let be, let be! Thou art
The armourer of my heart. False, false. This, this!

CLEOPATRA — Sooth, la, I'll help. Thus it must be.

ANTONY — Well, well,
We shall thrive now. Seest thou, my good fellow?
Go put on thy defences.

EROS — Briefly, sir.

CLEOPATRA — Is not this buckled well?

ANTONY — Rarely, rarely.
He that unbuckles this, till we do please
To daff't for our repose, shall hear a storm.
Thou fumblest, Eros, and my queen's a squire
More tight at this than thou. Dispatch. O love,
That thou couldst see my wars today, and

knew'st
The royal occupation, thou shouldst see
A workman in't.

Enter an OFFICER, *armed.*

Good morrow to thee. Welcome.
Thou look'st like him that knows a warlike charge.
To business that we love we rise betime
And go to't with delight.

OFFICER A thousand, sir,
Early though't be, have on their riveted trim
And at the port expect you.

[*Shout. Trumpets flourish.*]

Enter other CAPTAINS *and* SOLDIERS.

CAPTAIN The morn is fair. Good morrow, general.

ALL Good morrow, general.

ANTONY 'Tis well blown, lads.
This morning, like the spirit of a youth
That means to be of note, begins betimes.
So, so. Come, give me that. This way. Well said.
Fare thee well, dame.
Whate'er becomes of me,
This is a soldier's kiss. [*Kisses her.*] Rebukeable
And worthy shameful check it were, to stand
On more mechanic compliment. I'll leave thee
Now like a man of steel.—You that will fight,
Follow me close, I'll bring you to't. Adieu.

[*Exeunt* ANTONY, EROS, CAPTAINS *and* SOLDIERS.]

CHARMIAN Please you, retire to your chamber.

CLEOPATRA Lead me.
He goes forth gallantly. That he and Caesar might
Determine this great war in single fight!
Then Antony—but now—. Well, on.

[*Exeunt.*]

SCENE-V — Antony's camp near Alexandria

Trumpets sound. Enter ANTONY *and* EROS, *a* SOLDIER *meeting them.*

SOLDIER The gods make this a happy day to Antony!

ANTONY Would thou and those thy scars had once prevailed
To make me fight at land!

SOLDIER Hadst thou done so,
The kings that have revolted and the soldier
That has this morning left thee would have still
Followed thy heels.

ANTONY Who's gone this morning?

SOLDIER Who?
One ever near thee. Call for Enobarbus,
He shall not hear thee, or from Caesar's camp
Say "I am none of thine."

ANTONY What sayest thou?

SOLDIER Sir,
He is with Caesar.

EROS Sir, his chests and treasure
He has not with him.

ANTONY Is he gone?

SOLDIER Most certain.

ANTONY Go, Eros, send his treasure after. Do it.
Detain no jot, I charge thee. Write to him—
I will subscribe—gentle adieus and greetings.
Say that I wish he never find more cause
To change a master. O, my fortunes have
Corrupted honest men! Dispatch.—Enobarbus!

[*Exeunt.*]

SCENE-VI — Alexandria. Caesar's camp

Flourish. Enter AGRIPPA, CAESAR *with* ENOBARBUS *and* DOLABELLA.

CAESAR — Go forth, Agrippa, and begin the fight.
Our will is Antony be took alive;
Make it so known.

AGRIPPA — Caesar, I shall.

[*Exit.*]

CAESAR — The time of universal peace is near.
Prove this a prosp'rous day, the three-nooked world
Shall bear the olive freely.

Enter a MESSENGER.

MESSENGER — Antony
Is come into the field.

CAESAR — Go charge Agrippa
Plant those that have revolted in the van
That Antony may seem to spend his fury
Upon himself.

[*Exeunt* CAESAR *and his Train.*]

ENOBARBUS — Alexas did revolt and went to Jewry on
Affairs of Antony; there did dissuade
Great Herod to incline himself to Caesar
And leave his master Antony. For this pains
Casaer hath hanged him. Canidius and the rest
That fell away have entertainment but
No honourable trust. I have done ill,
Of which I do accuse myself so sorely
That I will joy no more.

Enter a SOLDIER *of* CAESAR'S.

SOLDIER Enobarbus, Antony
Hath after thee sent all thy treasure, with
His bounty overplus. The messenger
Came on my guard, and at thy tent is now
Unloading of his mules.

ENOBARBUS I give it you.

SOLDIER Mock not, Enobarbus.
I tell you true. Best you safed the bringer
Out of the host. I must attend mine office,
Or would have done't myself. Your emperor
Continues still a Jove.

[*Exit.*]

ENOBARBUS I am alone the villain of the earth,
And feel I am so most. O Antony,
Thou mine of bounty, how wouldst thou have paid
My better service, when my turpitude
Thou dost so crown with gold! This blows my heart.
If swift thought break it not, a swifter mean
Shall outstrike thought, but thought will do't, I feel.
I fight against thee! No, I will go seek
Some ditch wherein to die; the foul'st best fits
My latter part of life.

[*Exit.*]

SCENE-VII — Field of battle between the Camps

Alarum. DRUMS *and* TRUMPETS. *Enter* AGRIPPA *and others.*

AGRIPPA Retire! We have engaged ourselves too far.
Caesar himself has work, and our oppression
Exceeds what we expected.

[*Exeunt.*]

Alarums. Enter ANTONY *and* SCARUS *wounded.*

SCARUS O my brave emperor, this is fought indeed!
Had we done so at first, we had droven them home
With clouts about their heads.

ANTONY Thou bleed'st apace.

SCARUS I had a wound here that was like a T,
But now 'tis made an H.

Sounds retreat far off.

ANTONY They do retire.

SCARUS We'll beat 'em into bench-holes. I have yet
Room for six scotches more.

Enter EROS.

EROS They are beaten, sir, and our advantage serves
For a fair victory.

SCARUS Let us score their backs
And snatch 'em up as we take hares, behind.
'Tis sport to maul a runner.

ANTONY I will reward thee
Once for thy sprightly comfort, and tenfold
For thy good valour. Come thee on.

SCARUS I'll halt after.

[*Exeunt.*]

SCENE-VIII — Under the Walls of Alexandria

Alarum. Enter ANTONY *again in a march;* SCARUS *with others.*

ANTONY

We have beat him to his camp. Run one before
And let the Queen know of our gests.
Tomorrow,
Before the sun shall see's, we'll spill the blood
That has today escaped. I thank you all,
For doughty-handed are you, and have fought
Not as you served the cause, but as't had been
Each man's like mine. You have shown all
Hectors.
Enter the city, clip your wives, your friends,
Tell them your feats; whilst they with joyful
tears
Wash the congealment from your wounds and
kiss
The honoured gashes whole.

Enter CLEOPATRA.

[*To Scarus*.] Give me thy hand.
To this great fairy I'll commend thy acts,
Make her thanks bless thee. O thou day o' th'
world,
Chain mine armed neck. Leap thou, attire and
all,
Through proof of harness to my heart, and
there
Ride on the pants triumphing.

CLEOPATRA

Lord of lords!
O infinite virtue, com'st thou smiling from
The world's great snare uncaught?

ANTONY Mine nightingale,
We have beat them to their beds. What, girl! Though grey
Do something mingle with our younger brown, yet ha' we
A brain that nourishes our nerves and can
Get goal for goal of youth. Behold this man.
Commend unto his lips thy favouring hand.—
Kiss it, my warrior. He hath fought today
As if a god, in hate of mankind, had
Destroyed in such a shape.

CLEOPATRA I'll give thee, friend,
An armour all of gold. It was a king's.

ANTONY He has deserved it, were it carbuncled
Like holy Phœbus' car. Give me thy hand.
Through Alexandria make a jolly march;
Bear our hacked targets like the men that owe them.
Had our great palace the capacity
To camp this host, we all would sup together
And drink carouses to the next day's fate,
Which promises royal peril.—Trumpeters,
With brazen din blast you the city's ear;
Make mingle with our rattling tabourines,
That heaven and earth may strike their sounds together,
Applauding our approach.

[*Exeunt.*]

SCENE-IX — Caesar's camp

Enter a SENTRY *and his company.* ENOBARBUS *follows.*

SENTRY
If we be not relieved within this hour,
We must return to th' court of guard. The night
Is shiny, and they say we shall embattle
By th' second hour i' th' morn.

FIRST WATCH
This last day was a shrewd one to's.

ENOBARBUS
O, bear me witness, night.—

SECOND WATCH
What man is this?

FIRST WATCH
Stand close and list him.

ENOBARBUS
Be witness to me, O thou blessed moon,
When men revolted shall upon record
Bear hateful memory, poor Enobarbus did
Before thy face repent.

SENTRY
Enobarbus?

SECOND WATCH
Peace! Hark further.

ENOBARBUS
O sovereign mistress of true melancholy,
The poisonous damp of night disponge upon me,
That life, a very rebel to my will,
May hang no longer on me. Throw my heart
Against the flint and hardness of my fault,
Which, being dried with grief, will break to powder
And finish all foul thoughts. O Antony,
Nobler than my revolt is infamous,
Forgive me in thine own particular,
But let the world rank me in register
A master-leaver and a fugitive.
O Antony! O Antony!

[*Dies.*]

FIRST WATCH — Let's speak to him.

SENTRY — Let's hear him, for the things he speaks may concern Caesar.

SECOND WATCH — Let's do so. But he sleeps.

SENTRY — Swoons rather, for so bad a prayer as his
Was never yet for sleep.

FIRST WATCH — Go we to him.

SECOND WATCH — Awake, sir, awake! Speak to us.

FIRST WATCH — Hear you, sir?

SENTRY — The hand of death hath raught him.

[*Drums afar off.*]

Hark! The drums
Demurely wake the sleepers. Let us bear him
To th' court of guard; he is of note. Our hour
Is fully out.

SECOND WATCH — Come on, then. He may recover yet.

[*Exeunt with the body.*]

SCENE-X — Ground between the two Camps

Enter ANTONY *and* SCARUS *with their army.*

ANTONY

Their preparation is today by sea;
We please them not by land.

SCARUS

For both, my lord.

ANTONY

I would they'd fight i' th' fire or i' th' air;
We'd fight there too. But this it is: our foot
Upon the hills adjoining to the city
Shall stay with us—order for sea is given;
They have put forth the haven—
Where their appointment we may best discover
And look on their endeavour.

[*Exeunt.*]

SCENE-XI — Another part of the Ground

Enter CAESAR *and his army.*

CAESAR

But being charged, we will be still by land,
Which, as I take't, we shall, for his best force
Is forth to man his galleys. To the vales,
And hold our best advantage.

[*Exeunt.*]

SCENE-XII — Another part of the Ground

Alarum afar off, as at a sea fight. Enter ANTONY *and* SCARUS.

ANTONY
Yet they are not joined. Where yond pine does stand
I shall discover all. I'll bring thee word
Straight how 'tis like to go.

[*Exit.*]

SCARUS
Swallows have built
In Cleopatra's sails their nests. The augurs
Say they know not, they cannot tell; look grimly,
And dare not speak their knowledge. Antony
Is valiant and dejected, and by starts
His fretted fortunes give him hope and fear
Of what he has and has not.

Enter ANTONY.

ANTONY
All is lost!
This foul Egyptian hath betrayed me.
My fleet hath yielded to the foe, and yonder
They cast their caps up and carouse together
Like friends long lost. Triple-turned whore! 'Tis thou
Hast sold me to this novice, and my heart
Makes only wars on thee. Bid them all fly;
For when I am revenged upon my charm,
I have done all. Bid them all fly! Be gone!

[*Exit Scarus.*]

O sun, thy uprise shall I see no more.
Fortune and Antony part here; even here
Do we shake hands. All come to this! The hearts
That spanieled me at heels, to whom I gave

Their wishes, do discandy, melt their sweets
On blossoming Caesar, and this pine is barked
That overtopped them all. Betray'd I am:
O this false soul of Egypt! This grave charm,
Whose eye becked forth my wars and called them home,
Whose bosom was my crownet, my chief end,
Like a right gypsy hath at fast and loose
Beguiled me to the very heart of loss.
What, Eros, Eros!

Enter CLEOPATRA.

Ah, thou spell! Avaunt!

CLEOPATRA Why is my lord enraged against his love?

ANTONY Vanish, or I shall give thee thy deserving
And blemish Caesar's triumph. Let him take thee
And hoist thee up to the shouting plebeians!
Follow his chariot, like the greatest spot
Of all thy sex; most monster-like be shown
For poor'st diminutives, for dolts, and let
Patient Octavia plough thy visage up
With her prepared nails.

[*Exit* CLEOPATRA.]

'Tis well thou'rt gone,
If it be well to live; but better 'twere
Thou fell'st into my fury, for one death
Might have prevented many.—Eros, ho!—
The shirt of Nessus is upon me. Teach me,
Alcides, thou mine ancestor, thy rage.
Let me lodge Lichas on the horns o' th' moon,
And with those hands that grasped the heaviest club
Subdue my worthiest self. The witch shall die.
To the young Roman boy she hath sold me, and I fall
Under this plot. She dies for't.—Eros, ho!

[*Exit.*]

SCENE-XIII — Alexandria. A Room in the Palace

Enter CLEOPATRA, CHARMIAN, IRAS *and* MARDIAN.

CLEOPATRA
Help me, my women! O, he is more mad
Than Telamon for his shield; the boar of Thessaly
Was never so embossed.

CHARMIAN
To th' monument!
There lock yourself and send him word you are dead.
The soul and body rive not more in parting
Than greatness going off.

CLEOPATRA
To th' monument!
Mardian, go tell him I have slain myself.
Say that the last I spoke was "Antony",
And word it, prithee, piteously. Hence, Mardian,
And bring me how he takes my death.—To th' monument!

[*Exeunt.*]

SCENE-XIV — Alexandria. Another Room

Enter ANTONY *and* EROS.

ANTONY Eros, thou yet behold'st me?

EROS Ay, noble lord.

ANTONY Sometime we see a cloud that's dragonish,
A vapour sometime like a bear or lion,
A towered citadel, a pendant rock,
A forked mountain, or blue promontory
With trees upon't, that nod unto the world
And mock our eyes with air. Thou hast seen these signs.
They are black vesper's pageants.

EROS Ay, my lord.

ANTONY That which is now a horse, even with a thought
The rack dislimns and makes it indistinct
As water is in water.

EROS It does, my lord.

ANTONY My good knave Eros, now thy captain is
Even such a body. Here I am Antony,
Yet cannot hold this visible shape, my knave.
I made these wars for Egypt, and the Queen,
Whose heart I thought I had, for she had mine,
Which, whilst it was mine, had annexed unto't
A million more, now lost—she, Eros, has
Packed cards with Caesar, and false-played my glory
Unto an enemy's triumph.
Nay, weep not, gentle Eros. There is left us
Ourselves to end ourselves.

Enter MARDIAN.

O, thy vile lady!
She has robbed me of my sword.

MARDIAN
No, Antony,
My mistress loved thee and her fortunes mingled
With thine entirely.

ANTONY
Hence, saucy eunuch! Peace!
She hath betrayed me and shall die the death.

MARDIAN
Death of one person can be paid but once,
And that she has discharged. What thou wouldst do
Is done unto thy hand. The last she spake
Was "Antony! Most noble Antony!"
Then in the midst a tearing groan did break
The name of Antony; it was divided
Between her heart and lips. She rendered life,
Thy name so buried in her.

ANTONY
Dead, then?

MARDIAN
Dead.

ANTONY
Unarm, Eros. The long day's task is done,
And we must sleep.—That thou depart'st hence safe
Does pay thy labour richly. Go.

[*Exit* MARDIAN.]

Off, pluck off!
The sevenfold shield of Ajax cannot keep
The battery from my heart. O, cleave, my sides!
Heart, once be stronger than thy continent;
Crack thy frail case! Apace, Eros, apace!
No more a soldier. Bruised pieces, go;
You have been nobly borne. From me awhile.

[*Exit Eros.*]

I will o'ertake thee, Cleopatra, and
Weep for my pardon. So it must be, for now
All length is torture. Since the torch is out,

Lie down, and stray no farther. Now all labour
Mars what it does; yea, very force entangles
Itself with strength. Seal then, and all is done.
Eros!—I come, my queen.—Eros!—Stay for me.
Where souls do couch on flowers, we'll hand in hand,
And with our sprightly port make the ghosts gaze.
Dido and her Aeneas shall want troops,
And all the haunt be ours.—Come, Eros, Eros!

Enter EROS.

EROS
What would my lord?

ANTONY
Since Cleopatra died,
I have lived in such dishonour that the gods
Detest my baseness. I, that with my sword
Quartered the world, and o'er green Neptune's back
With ships made cities, condemn myself to lack
The courage of a woman; less noble mind
Than she which, by her death, our Caesar tells
"I am conqueror of myself." Thou art sworn, Eros,
That when the exigent should come, which now
Is come indeed, when I should see behind me
Th' inevitable prosecution of
Disgrace and horror, that on my command
Thou then wouldst kill me. Do't. The time is come.
Thou strik'st not me; 'tis Caesar thou defeat'st.
Put colour in thy cheek.

EROS
The gods withhold me!
Shall I do that which all the Parthian darts,
Though enemy, lost aim and could not?

ANTONY
Eros,
Wouldst thou be windowed in great Rome and see
Thy master thus with pleached arms, bending down

His corrigible neck, his face subdued
To penetrative shame, whilst the wheeled seat
Of fortunate Caesar, drawn before him, branded
His baseness that ensued?

EROS I would not see't.

ANTONY Come, then, for with a wound I must be cured.
Draw that thy honest sword, which thou hast worn
Most useful for thy country.

EROS O, sir, pardon me!

ANTONY When I did make thee free, swor'st thou not then
To do this when I bade thee? Do it at once,
Or thy precedent services are all
But accidents unpurposed. Draw, and come.

EROS Turn from me then that noble countenance
Wherein the worship of the whole world lies.

ANTONY Lo thee!

[*Turning from him.*]

EROS My sword is drawn.

ANTONY Then let it do at once
The thing why thou hast drawn it.

EROS My dear master,
My captain and my emperor, let me say,
Before I strike this bloody stroke, farewell.

ANTONY 'Tis said, man, and farewell.

EROS Farewell, great chief. Shall I strike now?

ANTONY Now, Eros.

EROS Why, there then! [*kills himself*]
Thus do I escape the sorrow
Of Antony's death.

[*Dies.*]

ANTONY Thrice nobler than myself!
Thou teachest me, O valiant Eros, what
I should and thou couldst not. My queen and Eros

Have by their brave instruction got upon me
A nobleness in record. But I will be
A bridegroom in my death and run into't
As to a lover's bed. Come then, and, Eros,
Thy master dies thy scholar. To do thus

[*Falling on his sword.*]

I learned of thee. How? Not dead? Not dead?
The guard, ho! O, dispatch me!

Enter a company of the GUARD, *one of them* DERCETUS.

FIRST GUARD What's the noise?

ANTONY I have done my work ill, friends. O, make an end
Of what I have begun.

SECOND GUARD The star is fallen.

FIRST GUARD And time is at his period.

ALL Alas, and woe!

ANTONY Let him that loves me strike me dead.

FIRST GUARD Not I.

SECOND GUARD Nor I.

THIRD GUARD Nor anyone.

[*Exeunt* GUARD.]

DERCETUS Thy death and fortunes bid thy followers fly.
This sword but shown to Caesar with this tidings,
Shall enter me with him.

Enter DIOMEDES.

DIOMEDES Where's Antony?

DERCETUS There, Diomed, there.

DIOMEDES Lives he? Wilt thou not answer, man?

[*Exit* DERCETUS.]

ANTONY Art thou there, Diomed? Draw thy sword and give me
Sufficing strokes for death.

DIOMEDES Most absolute lord,
My mistress Cleopatra sent me to thee.

ANTONY — When did she send thee?

DIOMEDES — Now, my lord.

ANTONY — Where is she?

DIOMEDES — Locked in her monument. She had a prophesying fear
Of what hath come to pass. For when she saw—
Which never shall be found—you did suspect
She had disposed with Caesar, and that your rage
Would not be purged, she sent you word she was dead;
But fearing since how it might work, hath sent
Me to proclaim the truth, and I am come,
I dread, too late.

ANTONY — Too late, good Diomed. Call my guard, I prithee.

DIOMEDES — What, ho! The emperor's guard! The guard, what ho!
Come, your lord calls!

Enter four or five of the GUARD *of* ANTONY.

ANTONY — Bear me, good friends, where Cleopatra bides.
'Tis the last service that I shall command you.

FIRST GUARD — Woe, woe are we, sir, you may not live to wear
All your true followers out.

ALL — Most heavy day!

ANTONY — Nay, good my fellows, do not please sharp fate
To grace it with your sorrows. Bid that welcome
Which comes to punish us, and we punish it,
Seeming to bear it lightly. Take me up.
I have led you oft; carry me now, good friends,
And have my thanks for all.

[*Exeunt, bearing* ANTONY.]

SCENE-XV — Alexandria. A monument

Enter CLEOPATRA *and her maids aloft, with* CHARMIAN *and* IRAS.

CLEOPATRA O Charmian, I will never go from hence.

CHARMIAN Be comforted, dear madam.

CLEOPATRA No, I will not.
All strange and terrible events are welcome,
But comforts we despise. Our size of sorrow,
Proportioned to our cause, must be as great
As that which makes it.

Enter, below DIOMEDES.

How now! Is he dead?

DIOMEDES His death's upon him, but not dead.
Look out o' th' other side your monument;
His guard have brought him thither.

Enter, below ANTONY *borne by the* GUARD.

CLEOPATRA O sun,
Burn the great sphere thou mov'st in! Darkling stand
The varying shore o' th' world. O Antony,
Antony, Antony! Help, Charmian! Help, Iras, help!
Help, friends below! Let's draw him hither.

ANTONY Peace!
Not Caesar's valour hath o'erthrown Antony,
But Antony's hath triumphed on itself.

CLEOPATRA So it should be, that none but Antony
Should conquer Antony, but woe 'tis so!

ANTONY I am dying, Egypt, dying. Only

I here importune death awhile until
Of many thousand kisses the poor last
I lay upon thy lips.

CLEOPATRA I dare not, dear
Dear my lord, pardon. I dare not,
Lest I be taken. Not th' imperious show
Of the full-fortuned Caesar ever shall
Be brooched with me; if knife, drugs, serpents, have
Edge, sting, or operation, I am safe.
Your wife Octavia, with her modest eyes
And still conclusion, shall acquire no honour
Demuring upon me. But come, come, Antony—
Help me, my women—we must draw thee up.
Assist, good friends.

ANTONY O, quick, or I am gone.

CLEOPATRA Here's sport indeed! How heavy weighs my lord!
Our strength is all gone into heaviness;
That makes the weight. Had I great Juno's power,
The strong-winged Mercury should fetch thee up
And set thee by Jove's side. Yet come a little;
Wishers were ever fools. O come, come come,

[*They heave* ANTONY *aloft to* CLEOPATRA.]

And welcome, welcome! Die where thou hast lived;
Quicken with kissing. Had my lips that power,
Thus would I wear them out.

ALL A heavy sight!

ANTONY I am dying, Egypt, dying.
Give me some wine, and let me speak a little.

CLEOPATRA No, let me speak, and let me rail so high
That the false huswife Fortune break her wheel,
Provoked by my offence.

ANTONY One word, sweet queen:
Of Caesar seek your honour, with your safety.
O!

CLEOPATRA They do not go together.

ANTONY Gentle, hear me.
None about Caesar trust but Proculeius.

CLEOPATRA My resolution and my hands I'll trust;
None about Caesar.

ANTONY The miserable change now at my end
Lament nor sorrow at, but please your thoughts
In feeding them with those my former fortunes
Wherein I lived the greatest prince o' th' world,
The noblest; and do now not basely die,
Not cowardly put off my helmet to
My countryman; a Roman by a Roman
Valiantly vanquished. Now my spirit is going;
I can no more.

CLEOPATRA Noblest of men, woo't die?
Hast thou no care of me? Shall I abide
In this dull world, which in thy absence is
No better than a sty? O, see, my women,

[ANTONY DIES.]

The crown o' th' earth doth melt.—My lord!
O, withered is the garland of the war,
The soldier's pole is fallen; young boys and girls
Are level now with men. The odds is gone,
And there is nothing left remarkable
Beneath the visiting moon.

[*Faints.*]

CHARMIAN O, quietness, lady!

IRAS She is dead too, our sovereign.

CHARMIAN Lady!

IRAS Madam!

CHARMIAN O madam, madam, madam!

IRAS Royal Egypt, Empress!

CHARMIAN Peace, peace, Iras!

CLEOPATRA No more but e'en a woman, and commanded
By such poor passion as the maid that milks
And does the meanest chares. It were for me

To throw my sceptre at the injurious gods,
To tell them that this world did equal theirs
Till they had stolen our jewel. All's but naught;
Patience is sottish, and impatience does
Become a dog that's mad. Then is it sin
To rush into the secret house of death
Ere death dare come to us? How do you,
women?
What, what! good cheer! Why, how now,
Charmian?
My noble girls! Ah, women, women! Look,
Our lamp is spent, it's out! Good sirs, take
heart.
We'll bury him; and then, what's brave, what's
noble,
Let's do it after the high Roman fashion
And make death proud to take us. Come, away.
This case of that huge spirit now is cold.
Ah, women, women! Come, we have no friend
But resolution and the briefest end.

[*Exeunt, bearing off* ANTONY'S *body.*]

ACT-V
SCENE-I — Caesar's Camp before Alexandria

Enter CAESAR, AGRIPPA, DOLABELLA, MAECENAS, GALLUS, PROCULEIUS *with his council of war.*

CAESAR
Go to him, Dolabella, bid him yield.
Being so frustrate, tell him, he mocks
The pauses that he makes.

DOLABELLA
Caesar, I shall.

[*Exit.*]

Enter DERCETUS *with the sword of* ANTONY.

CAESAR
Wherefore is that? And what art thou that dar'st
Appear thus to us?

DERCETUS
I am called Dercetus.
Mark Antony I served, who best was worthy
Best to be served. Whilst he stood up and spoke,
He was my master, and I wore my life
To spend upon his haters. If thou please
To take me to thee, as I was to him
I'll be to Caesar; if thou pleasest not,
I yield thee up my life.

CAESAR
What is't thou say'st?

DERCETUS
I say, O Caesar, Antony is dead.

CAESAR
The breaking of so great a thing should make
A greater crack. The round world
Should have shook lions into civil streets,
And citizens to their dens. The death of Antony
Is not a single doom; in the name lay
A moiety of the world.

DERCETUS He is dead, Caesar,
Not by a public minister of justice,
Nor by a hired knife, but that self hand
Which writ his honour in the acts it did
Hath, with the courage which the heart did lend it,
Splitted the heart. This is his sword.
I robbed his wound of it. Behold it stained
With his most noble blood.

CAESAR Look you sad, friends?
The gods rebuke me, but it is tidings
To wash the eyes of kings.

AGRIPPA And strange it is
That nature must compel us to lament
Our most persisted deeds.

MAECENAS His taints and honours
Waged equal with him.

AGRIPPA A rarer spirit never
Did steer humanity, but you gods will give us
Some faults to make us men. Caesar is touched.

MAECENAS When such a spacious mirror's set before him,
He needs must see himself.

CAESAR O Antony,
I have followed thee to this, but we do lance
Diseases in our bodies. I must perforce
Have shown to thee such a declining day
Or look on thine. We could not stall together
In the whole world. But yet let me lament
With tears as sovereign as the blood of hearts,
That thou, my brother, my competitor
In top of all design, my mate in empire,
Friend and companion in the front of war,
The arm of mine own body, and the heart
Where mine his thoughts did kindle, that our stars,
Unreconciliable, should divide
Our equalness to this. Hear me, good friends—

Enter an EGYPTIAN.

But I will tell you at some meeter season.
The business of this man looks out of him;
We'll hear him what he says. Whence are you?

EGYPTIAN A poor Egyptian yet. The queen, my mistress,
Confined in all she has, her monument,
Of thy intents desires instruction,
That she preparedly may frame herself
To the way she's forced to.

CAESAR Bid her have good heart.
She soon shall know of us, by some of ours,
How honourable and how kindly we
Determine for her. For Caesar cannot lean
To be ungentle.

EGYPTIAN So the gods preserve thee!

[*Exit.*]

CAESAR Come hither, Proculeius. Go and say
We purpose her no shame. Give her what comforts
The quality of her passion shall require,
Lest, in her greatness, by some mortal stroke
She do defeat us, for her life in Rome
Would be eternal in our triumph. Go,
And with your speediest bring us what she says
And how you find of her.

PROCULEIUS Caesar, I shall.

[*Exit* PROCULEIUS.]

CAESAR Gallus, go you along.

[*Exit* GALLUS.]

Where's Dolabella, to second Proculeius?

ALL Dolabella!

CAESAR Let him alone, for I remember now
How he's employed. He shall in time be ready.
Go with me to my tent, where you shall see
How hardly I was drawn into this war,
How calm and gentle I proceeded still
In all my writings. Go with me and see
What I can show in this.

[*Exeunt.*]

SCENE-II — Alexandria. A Room in the Monument

Enter CLEOPATRA, CHARMIAN *and* IRAS.

CLEOPATRA
My desolation does begin to make
A better life. 'Tis paltry to be Caesar;
Not being Fortune, he's but Fortune's knave,
A minister of her will. And it is great
To do that thing that ends all other deeds,
Which shackles accidents and bolts up change,
Which sleeps and never palates more the dung,
The beggar's nurse and Caesar's.

Enter PROCULEIUS.

PROCULEIUS
Caesar sends greetings to the queen of Egypt,
And bids thee study on what fair demands
Thou mean'st to have him grant thee.

CLEOPATRA
What's thy name?

PROCULEIUS
My name is Proculeius.

CLEOPATRA
Antony
Did tell me of you, bade me trust you, but
I do not greatly care to be deceived
That have no use for trusting. If your master
Would have a queen his beggar, you must tell him
That majesty, to keep decorum, must
No less beg than a kingdom. If he please
To give me conquered Egypt for my son,
He gives me so much of mine own as I
Will kneel to him with thanks.

PROCULEIUS
Be of good cheer.
You are fallen into a princely hand; fear nothing.

Make your full reference freely to my lord,
Who is so full of grace that it flows over
On all that need. Let me report to him
Your sweet dependency, and you shall find
A conqueror that will pray in aid for kindness
Where he for grace is kneeled to.

CLEOPATRA Pray you tell him
I am his fortune's vassal and I send him
The greatness he has got. I hourly learn
A doctrine of obedience, and would gladly
Look him i' th' face.

PROCULEIUS This I'll report, dear lady.
Have comfort, for I know your plight is pitied
Of him that caused it.

Enter GALLUS *and Roman* SOLDIERS.

You see how easily she may be surprised.
Guard her till Caesar come.

IRAS Royal queen!

CHARMIAN O Cleopatra, thou art taken, queen!

CLEOPATRA Quick, quick, good hands.

[*Drawing a dagger.*]

PROCULEIUS Hold, worthy lady, hold!

[*Seizes and disarms her.*]

Do not yourself such wrong, who are in this
Relieved, but not betrayed.

CLEOPATRA What, of death too,
That rids our dogs of languish?

PROCULEIUS Cleopatra,
Do not abuse my master's bounty by
Th' undoing of yourself. Let the world see
His nobleness well acted, which your death
Will never let come forth.

CLEOPATRA Where art thou, Death?
Come hither, come! Come, come, and take a
queen
Worth many babes and beggars!

PROCULEIUS — O, temperance, lady!

CLEOPATRA — Sir, I will eat no meat; I'll not drink, sir;
If idle talk will once be necessary,
I'll not sleep neither. This mortal house I'll ruin,
Do Caesar what he can. Know, sir, that I
Will not wait pinioned at your master's court,
Nor once be chastised with the sober eye
Of dull Octavia. Shall they hoist me up
And show me to the shouting varletry
Of censuring Rome? Rather a ditch in Egypt
Be gentle grave unto me! Rather on Nilus' mud
Lay me stark-naked, and let the water-flies
Blow me into abhorring! Rather make
My country's high pyramides my gibbet
And hang me up in chains!

PROCULEIUS — You do extend
These thoughts of horror further than you shall
Find cause in Caesar.

Enter DOLABELLA.

DOLABELLA — Proculeius,
What thou hast done thy master Caesar knows,
And he hath sent for thee. For the queen,
I'll take her to my guard.

PROCULEIUS — So, Dolabella,
It shall content me best. Be gentle to her.
[*To Cleopatra.*] To Caesar I will speak what you shall please,
If you'll employ me to him.

CLEOPATRA — Say I would die.

[*Exeunt* PROCULEIUS *and* SOLDIERS.]

DOLABELLA — Most noble empress, you have heard of me?

CLEOPATRA — I cannot tell.

DOLABELLA — Assuredly you know me.

CLEOPATRA — No matter, sir, what I have heard or known.
You laugh when boys or women tell their dreams;
Is't not your trick?

DOLABELLA I understand not, madam.

CLEOPATRA I dreamt there was an Emperor Antony.
O, such another sleep, that I might see
But such another man!

DOLABELLA If it might please you—

CLEOPATRA His face was as the heavens, and therein stuck
A sun and moon, which kept their course, and lighted
The little O, the earth.

DOLABELLA Most sovereign creature—

CLEOPATRA His legs bestrid the ocean; his reared arm
Crested the world; his voice was propertied
As all the tuned spheres, and that to friends;
But when he meant to quail and shake the orb,
He was as rattling thunder. For his bounty,
There was no winter in't; an autumn 'twas
That grew the more by reaping. His delights
Were dolphin-like; they showed his back above
The element they lived in. In his livery
Walked crowns and crownets; realms and islands were
As plates dropped from his pocket.

DOLABELLA Cleopatra—

CLEOPATRA Think you there was or might be such a man
As this I dreamt of?

DOLABELLA Gentle madam, no.

CLEOPATRA You lie up to the hearing of the gods!
But if there be nor ever were one such,
It's past the size of dreaming. Nature wants stuff
To vie strange forms with fancy; yet t' imagine
An Antony were nature's piece 'gainst fancy,
Condemning shadows quite.

DOLABELLA Hear me, good madam.
Your loss is, as yourself, great; and you bear it
As answering to the weight. Would I might never
O'ertake pursued success, but I do feel,

By the rebound of yours, a grief that smites
My very heart at root.

CLEOPATRA I thank you, sir.
Know you what Caesar means to do with me?

DOLABELLA I am loath to tell you what I would you knew.

CLEOPATRA Nay, pray you, sir.

DOLABELLA Though he be honourable—

CLEOPATRA He'll lead me, then, in triumph.

DOLABELLA Madam, he will. I know it.

Flourish. Enter CAESAR, PROCULEIUS, GALLUS, MAECENAS *and others of his train.*

ALL Make way there! Caesar!

CAESAR Which is the Queen of Egypt?

DOLABELLA It is the Emperor, madam.

[CLEOPATRA KNEELS.]

CAESAR Arise, you shall not kneel.
I pray you, rise. Rise, Egypt.

CLEOPATRA Sir, the gods
Will have it thus. My master and my lord
I must obey.

CAESAR Take to you no hard thoughts.
The record of what injuries you did us,
Though written in our flesh, we shall remember
As things but done by chance.

CLEOPATRA Sole sir o' th' world,
I cannot project mine own cause so well
To make it clear, but do confess I have
Been laden with like frailties which before
Have often shamed our sex.

CAESAR Cleopatra, know
We will extenuate rather than enforce.
If you apply yourself to our intents,
Which towards you are most gentle, you shall find
A benefit in this change; but if you seek
To lay on me a cruelty by taking

Antony's course, you shall bereave yourself
Of my good purposes, and put your children
To that destruction which I'll guard them from
If thereon you rely. I'll take my leave.

CLEOPATRA And may, through all the world. 'Tis yours, and we,
Your scutcheons and your signs of conquest, shall
Hang in what place you please. Here, my good lord.

CAESAR You shall advise me in all for Cleopatra.

CLEOPATRA This is the brief of money, plate, and jewels
I am possessed of. 'Tis exactly valued,
Not petty things admitted. Where's Seleucus?

Enter SELEUCUS.

SELEUCUS Here, madam.

CLEOPATRA This is my treasurer. Let him speak, my lord,
Upon his peril, that I have reserved
To myself nothing. Speak the truth, Seleucus.

SELEUCUS Madam, I had rather seal my lips
Than to my peril speak that which is not.

CLEOPATRA What have I kept back?

SELEUCUS Enough to purchase what you have made known.

CAESAR Nay, blush not, Cleopatra. I approve
Your wisdom in the deed.

CLEOPATRA See, Caesar! O, behold,
How pomp is followed! Mine will now be yours
And should we shift estates, yours would be mine.
The ingratitude of this Seleucus does
Even make me wild. O slave, of no more trust
Than love that's hired! What, goest thou back? Thou shalt
Go back, I warrant thee! But I'll catch thine eyes
Though they had wings. Slave, soulless villain, dog!
O rarely base!

CAESAR Good queen, let us entreat you.

CLEOPATRA O Caesar, what a wounding shame is this,
That thou vouchsafing here to visit me,
Doing the honour of thy lordliness
To one so meek, that mine own servant should
Parcel the sum of my disgraces by
Addition of his envy! Say, good Caesar,
That I some lady trifles have reserved,
Immoment toys, things of such dignity
As we greet modern friends withal; and say
Some nobler token I have kept apart
For Livia and Octavia, to induce
Their mediation, must I be unfolded
With one that I have bred? The gods! It smites me
Beneath the fall I have.
[*To Seleucus.*] Prithee go hence,
Or I shall show the cinders of my spirits
Through th' ashes of my chance. Wert thou a man,
Thou wouldst have mercy on me.

CAESAR Forbear, Seleucus.

[*Exit* SELEUCUS.]

CLEOPATRA Be it known that we, the greatest, are misthought
For things that others do; and when we fall,
We answer others' merits in our name,
Are therefore to be pitied.

CAESAR Cleopatra,
Not what you have reserved nor what acknowledged
Put we i' th' roll of conquest. Still be't yours;
Bestow it at your pleasure, and believe
Caesar's no merchant to make prize with you
Of things that merchants sold. Therefore be cheered;
Make not your thoughts your prisons. No, dear queen;
For we intend so to dispose you as

Yourself shall give us counsel. Feed and sleep.
Our care and pity is so much upon you
That we remain your friend; and so, adieu.

CLEOPATRA — My master and my lord!

CAESAR — Not so. Adieu.

[*Flourish. Exeunt* CAESAR *and his train.*]

CLEOPATRA — He words me, girls, he words me, that I should not
Be noble to myself. But hark thee, Charmian!

[*Whispers to* CHARMIAN.]

IRAS — Finish, good lady. The bright day is done,
And we are for the dark.

CLEOPATRA — Hie thee again.
I have spoke already, and it is provided.
Go put it to the haste.

CHARMIAN — Madam, I will.

Enter DOLABELLA.

DOLABELLA — Where's the Queen?

CHARMIAN — Behold, sir.

[*Exit.*]

CLEOPATRA — Dolabella!

DOLABELLA — Madam, as thereto sworn by your command,
Which my love makes religion to obey,
I tell you this: Caesar through Syria
Intends his journey, and within three days
You with your children will he send before.
Make your best use of this. I have performed
Your pleasure and my promise.

CLEOPATRA — Dolabella,
I shall remain your debtor.

DOLABELLA — I your servant.
Adieu, good queen. I must attend on Caesar.

CLEOPATRA — Farewell, and thanks.

[*Exit* DOLABELLA.]

Now, Iras, what think'st thou?

Thou an Egyptian puppet shall be shown
In Rome as well as I. Mechanic slaves
With greasy aprons, rules, and hammers shall
Uplift us to the view. In their thick breaths,
Rank of gross diet, shall we be enclouded,
And forced to drink their vapour.

IRAS The gods forbid!

CLEOPATRA Nay, 'tis most certain, Iras. Saucy lictors
Will catch at us like strumpets, and scald rhymers
Ballad us out o' tune. The quick comedians
Extemporally will stage us and present
Our Alexandrian revels; Antony
Shall be brought drunken forth, and I shall see
Some squeaking Cleopatra boy my greatness
I' th' posture of a whore.

IRAS O the good gods!

CLEOPATRA Nay, that's certain.

IRAS I'll never see't, for I am sure mine nails
Are stronger than mine eyes.

CLEOPATRA Why, that's the way
To fool their preparation and to conquer
Their most absurd intents.

Enter CHARMIAN.

Now, Charmian!
Show me, my women, like a queen. Go fetch
My best attires. I am again for Cydnus
To meet Mark Antony. Sirrah, Iras, go.
Now, noble Charmian, we'll dispatch indeed,
And when thou hast done this chare, I'll give thee leave
To play till doomsday. Bring our crown and all.

[*Exit* IRAS. *A noise within.*]

Wherefore's this noise?

Enter a GUARDSMAN.

GUARDSMAN Here is a rural fellow
That will not be denied your highness' presence.

He brings you figs.

CLEOPATRA Let him come in.

[*Exit* GUARDSMAN.]

What poor an instrument
May do a noble deed! He brings me liberty.
My resolution's placed, and I have nothing
Of woman in me. Now from head to foot
I am marble-constant. Now the fleeting moon
No planet is of mine.

Enter GUARDSMAN *and* CLOWN *with a basket.*

GUARDSMAN This is the man.

CLEOPATRA Avoid, and leave him.

[*Exit* GUARDSMAN.]

Hast thou the pretty worm of Nilus there
That kills and pains not?

CLOWN Truly, I have him, but I would not be the party that should desire you to touch him, for his biting is immortal. Those that do die of it do seldom or never recover.

CLEOPATRA Remember'st thou any that have died on't?

CLOWN Very many, men and women too. I heard of one of them no longer than yesterday—a very honest woman, but something given to lie; as a woman should not do but in the way of honesty—how she died of the biting of it, what pain she felt. Truly she makes a very good report o' th' worm; but he that will believe all that they say shall never be saved by half that they do. But this is most falliable, the worm's an odd worm.

CLEOPATRA Get thee hence. Farewell.

CLOWN I wish you all joy of the worm.

[*Sets down the basket.*]

CLEOPATRA Farewell.

CLOWN You must think this, look you, that the worm will do his kind.

CLEOPATRA — Ay, ay, farewell.

CLOWN — Look you, the worm is not to be trusted but in the keeping of wise people; for indeed there is no goodness in the worm.

CLEOPATRA — Take thou no care; it shall be heeded.

CLOWN — Very good. Give it nothing, I pray you, for it is not worth the feeding.

CLEOPATRA — Will it eat me?

CLOWN — You must not think I am so simple but I know the devil himself will not eat a woman. I know that a woman is a dish for the gods if the devil dress her not. But truly, these same whoreson devils do the gods great harm in their women, for in every ten that they make, the devils mar five.

CLEOPATRA — Well, get thee gone. Farewell.

CLOWN — Yes, forsooth. I wish you joy o' th' worm.

[*Exit.*]

Enter IRAS *with a robe, crown, &c.*

CLEOPATRA — Give me my robe. Put on my crown. I have
Immortal longings in me. Now no more
The juice of Egypt's grape shall moist this lip.
Yare, yare, good Iras; quick. Methinks I hear
Antony call. I see him rouse himself
To praise my noble act. I hear him mock
The luck of Caesar, which the gods give men
To excuse their after wrath. Husband, I come!
Now to that name my courage prove my title!
I am fire and air; my other elements
I give to baser life.—So, have you done?
Come then, and take the last warmth of my lips.
Farewell, kind Charmian. Iras, long farewell.

[*Kisses them.* IRAS *falls and dies.*]

Have I the aspic in my lips? Dost fall?
If thou and nature can so gently part,
The stroke of death is as a lover's pinch,

Which hurts and is desired. Dost thou lie still?
If thus thou vanishest, thou tell'st the world
It is not worth leave-taking.

CHARMIAN Dissolve, thick cloud, and rain, that I may say
The gods themselves do weep!

CLEOPATRA This proves me base.
If she first meet the curled Antony,
He'll make demand of her, and spend that kiss
Which is my heaven to have.—Come, thou mortal wretch,

[*To an asp, which she applies to her breast.*]

With thy sharp teeth this knot intrinsicate
Of life at once untie. Poor venomous fool,
Be angry and dispatch. O couldst thou speak,
That I might hear thee call great Caesar ass
Unpolicied!

CHARMIAN O eastern star!

CLEOPATRA Peace, peace!
Dost thou not see my baby at my breast
That sucks the nurse asleep?

CHARMIAN O, break! O, break!

CLEOPATRA As sweet as balm, as soft as air, as gentle—
O Antony!—Nay, I will take thee too.

[*Applying another asp to her arm.*]

What should I stay—

[*Dies.*]

CHARMIAN In this vile world? So, fare thee well.
Now boast thee, Death, in thy possession lies
A lass unparalleled. Downy windows, close,
And golden Phœbus never be beheld
Of eyes again so royal! Your crown's awry;
I'll mend it and then play.

Enter the GUARD *rustling in.*

FIRST GUARD Where's the queen?

CHARMIAN Speak softly. Wake her not.

FIRST GUARD Caesar hath sent—

CHARMIAN Too slow a messenger.

[*Applies an asp.*]

O, come apace, dispatch! I partly feel thee.

FIRST GUARD Approach, ho! All's not well. Caesar's beguiled.

SECOND GUARD There's Dolabella sent from Caesar. Call him.

FIRST GUARD What work is here, Charmian? Is this well done?

CHARMIAN It is well done, and fitting for a princess
Descended of so many royal kings.
Ah, soldier!

[CHARMIAN DIES.]

Enter DOLABELLA.

DOLABELLA How goes it here?

SECOND GUARD All dead.

DOLABELLA Caesar, thy thoughts
Touch their effects in this. Thyself art coming
To see performed the dreaded act which thou
So sought'st to hinder.

Enter CAESAR *and all his train, marching.*

ALL A way there, a way for Caesar!

DOLABELLA O sir, you are too sure an augurer:
That you did fear is done.

CAESAR Bravest at the last,
She levelled at our purposes and, being royal,
Took her own way. The manner of their deaths?
I do not see them bleed.

DOLABELLA Who was last with them?

FIRST GUARD A simple countryman that brought her figs.
This was his basket.

CAESAR Poisoned then.

FIRST GUARD O Caesar,
This Charmian lived but now; she stood and spake.
I found her trimming up the diadem
On her dead mistress; tremblingly she stood,
And on the sudden dropped.

CAESAR O noble weakness!
If they had swallowed poison 'twould appear
By external swelling; but she looks like sleep,
As she would catch another Antony
In her strong toil of grace.

DOLABELLA Here on her breast
There is a vent of blood, and something blown.
The like is on her arm.

FIRST GUARD This is an aspic's trail, and these fig leaves
Have slime upon them, such as th' aspic leaves
Upon the caves of Nile.

CAESAR Most probable
That so she died, for her physician tells me
She hath pursued conclusions infinite
Of easy ways to die. Take up her bed,
And bear her women from the monument.
She shall be buried by her Antony.
No grave upon the earth shall clip in it
A pair so famous. High events as these
Strike those that make them; and their story is
No less in pity than his glory which
Brought them to be lamented. Our army shall
In solemn show attend this funeral,
And then to Rome. Come, Dolabella, see
High order in this great solemnity.

[*Exeunt omnes.*]

* * *

www.ingramcontent.com/pod-product-compliance
Ingram Content Group UK Ltd.
Pitfield, Milton Keynes, MK11 3LW, UK
UKHW042016190726
13854UKWH00005B/2313